Blurt, Master Constable by Thomas Dekker
or The Spaniard's Night Walk

This play is also attributed as in collaboration with Thomas Middleton

— Patresq; severi
Fronde comas vincti coenant, et carmina dictant.

Thomas Dekker is a playwright, pamphleteer and poet who perhaps deserves greater recognition than he has so far gained.

Despite the fact only perhaps twenty of his plays were published, and fewer still survive, he was far more prolific than that. Born around 1572 his peak years were the mid 1590's to the 1620's – seven of which he spent in a debtor's prison. His works span the late Elizabethan and Caroline eras and his numerous collaborations with Ford, Middleton, Webster and Jonson say much about his work.

His pamphlets detail much of the life in these times, times of great change, of plague and of course that great capital city London a swirling mass of people, power, intrigue.

Index of Contents
Dramatis Personae
Act I
Scene I. A Room in Camillo's House
Scene II. A street before Blurt's House
Act II
Scene I. Outside a Tennis Court
Scene II. A Room in Imperia's House
Act III
Scene I. A Street before Hipolito's House
Scene II. An Old Chapel
Scene III. A Room in Imperia's House
Act IV
Scene I. A Street Before Imperia's House
Scene II. Lazarillo's Room in Imperia's House
Scene III. A Street Before Imperia's House
Act V
Scene I. A Room in Camillo's House
Scene II. A Room in Imperia's House
Scene III. A Street Before Imperia's House
Thomas Dekker – A Short Biography
Thomas Dekker – A Concise Bibliography

DRAMATIS PERSONAE
(in order of appearance)
HIPOLITO, a Venetian gentleman
VIOLETTA, his sister
FIRST LADY, called Hero
VIRGILIO, a Venetian gentleman
THIRD LADY
CAMILLO, a Venetian gentleman in love with Violetta
SECOND LADY
BAPTISTA, a Venetian gentleman
BENTIVOLIO, a Venetian gentleman
DOYT, Hipolito's page
DANDIPRAT, Camillo's page
FONTINELL, a French gentleman
LAZARILLO de Tormes de Castille, a Spanish soldier
PILCHER, his boy
BLURT, master constable
SLUBBER, his beadle
TRUEPENNY, Violetta's page
Serving-men
IMPERIA, a courtesan
TRIVIA, her maid
SIMPERINA, her maid
FRISCO, her porter
CURVETTO, an old courtier
MUSICIANS
A FRIAR
Five COURTESANS of Imperia's house
WOODCOCK, part of the watch
GULCH, part of the watch
ASORINO, a Venetian gentleman
The DUKE of Venice
KILDERKIN, part of the watch
PISSBREECH, part of the watch
CUCKOO, part of the watch
GARLIC, part of the watch

ACT I

SCENE I. A Room in Camillo's House

Enter CAMILLO with VIOLETTA, HIPOLITO, BAPTISTO, BENTIVOLIO, and VIRGILIO, as returning from war, everyone with a glove in his hat, VIOLETTA and ladies with them, DOYT and DANDIPRAT.

HIPOLITO
Ay, marry, sir, the only rising up in arms is in the arms of a woman: Peace, I say still, is your only paradise, when every Adam may have his Christmas Eve. And you take me lying any more by the cold sides of a brazen-face field-piece, unless I have such a down pillow under me, I'll give you leave to knock up both my golls in my father's hall, and hang hats upon these tenpenny nails.

VIOLETTA
And yet, brother, when with the sharpest hooks of my wit I labour'd to pull you from the wars, you broke loose, like a horse that knew his own strength, and vow'd nothing but a man of war should back you.

HIPOLITO
I have been back'd since and almost unback'd too.

VIOLETTA
And swore that honour was never dyed in grain till it was dipp'd in the colours of the field.

HIPOLITO
I am a new man, sister, and now cry a pox a' that honour, that must have none but barber-surgeons to wait upon't, and a band of poor straggling rascals, that every twinkling of an eye, forfeit their legs and arms into the Lord's hands. Wenches, by Mars his sweaty buff-jerkin (for now all my oaths must smell a' the soldado), I have seen more men's heads spurn'd up and down like footballs at a breakfast, after the hungry cannons had pick'd them, than are maidenheads in Venice, and more legs of men serv'd in at a dinner than ever I shall see legs of capons in one platter whilst I live.

FIRST LADY
Perhaps all those were capons' legs you did see.

VIRGILIO
Nay, mistress, I'll witness against you for some of them.

VIOLETTA
I do not think for all this that my brother stood to it so lustily as he makes his brags for.

THIRD LADY
No, no, these great talkers are never great doers.

VIOLETTA
Faith, brother, how many did you kill for your share?

HIPOLITO
Not so many as thou hast done with that villainous eye by a thousand.

VIOLETTA
I thought so much; that's just none.

CAMILLO

'Tis not a soldier's glory to tell how many lives he has ended, but how many he has saved: in both which honours the noble Hipolito had most excellent possession. Believe it, my fair mistress, tho' many men in a battle have done more, your brother in this equal'd him who did most. He went from you a worthy gentleman; he brings with him that title that makes a gentleman most worthy, the name of a soldier, which how well and how soon he hath earn'd would in me seem glorious to rehearse, in you to hear, but because his own ear dwells so near my voice, I will play the ill neighbour and case to speak well of him.

VIOLETTA
An argument that either you dare not or love not to flatter.

CAMILLO
No more than I dare or love to do wrong; yet to make a chronicle of my friend's nobly-acted deeds would stand as far from flattery in me as cowardice did from him.

HIPOLITO
'Sfoot, if all the wit in this company have nothing to set itself about but to run division upon me, why then e'en burn off mine ears indeed; but, my little mermaids, Signior Camillo does this that I now might describe the Ninevitical motion of the whole battle, and so tell what he has done. And come, shall I begin?

FIRST LADY
O, for beauty's love, a good motion.

HIPOLITO
But I can tell you one thing, I shall make your hair stand up an end at some things.

VIOLETTA
Prithee, good brother soldier, keep the peace. Our hair stand an end? Pity a' my heart, the next end would be of our wits; we hang out a white flag, most terrible Tamburlaine, and beg mercy. Come, come, let us neither have your Ninevitcal motions nor your swaggering battles. Why, my Lord Camillo, you invited me hither to a banquet, not to the ballad of a pitch'd field.

CAMILLO
And here it stands, bright mistress, sweetly attending what doom your lips will lay upon it.

VIOLETTA
Ay, marry, sir, let our teeth describe this motion.

SECOND LADY
We shall never describe it well for fumbling i' th' mouth.

HIPOLITO
Yes, yes, I have a trick to make us understand one another and we fumble never so—

VIOLETTA
Meddle not with his tricks, sweet heart. Under pardon, my lord, tho' I am your guest, I'll bestow myself. Sit, dear beauties: for the men, let them take up places themselves. I prithee, brother fighter, sit, and talk of any subject but this jangling law at arms.

HIPOLITO
The law at legs then.

VIOLETTA
Will you be so lusty? No, nor legs neither; we'll them tied up too. Since you are among ladies, gallants, handle those things only that are fit for ladies.

HIPOLITO
Agreed, so that we go not out of the compass of those things are fit for lords.

VIOLETTA
Be't so; what's the theme then?

FIRST LADY
Beauty; that fits us best.

CAMILLO
And of beauty what tongue would not speak the best, since it is the jewel that hangs upon the brow of heaven, the best colour that can be laid upon the cheek of earth? Beauty makes men gods immortal by making mortal men to live ever in love.

SECOND LADY
Ever? Not so; I have heard that some men have died for love.

VIOLETTA
So have I, but I could never see't. I'd ride forty miles to follow such a fellow to church, and would make more of a sprig of rosemary at his burial than of a gilded bride-branch at mine own wedding.

CAMILLO
Take you such delight in men that die for love?

VIOLETTA
Not in the men nor in the death, but in the deed. Troth, I think he is not a sound man that will die for a woman, and yet I would never love a man soundly that would not knock at death's door for my love.

HIPOLITO
I'd knock as long as I thought good, but have my brains knock'd out when I enter'd, if I were he.

CAMILLO
What Venetian gentleman was there that having this in his burgonet did not, to prove his head worthy of the honour, do more than defy death to the very face? Trust us, ladies, our signiory stands bound in greater sums of thanks to your beauties for victory than to our valor. My dear Violetta, one kiss to this picture of your whitest hand, when I was even faint with giving and receiving the dole of war,
Set a new edge on my sword, insomuch that
I singled out a gallant spirit of France,
And charg'd him with my lance in full career;
And after rich exchange of noble courage

The space of a good hour on either side,
At last crying, "Now for Violetta's honour!"
I vanquish'd him, and him dismounted took
Not to myself, but prisoner to my love.

VIOLETTA
I have heard much praise of that French gallant; good my lord, bring him acquainted with our eyes.

CAMILLO
I will. Go, boy, fetch noble Fontinell.

Exit DANDIPRAT.

HIPOLITO
Will your French prisoner drink well? Or else, cut his throat.

CAMILLO
Oh no, he cannot brook it.

HIPOLITO
The pox he can! 'Slight, methinks a Frenchman should have a good courage to wine, for many of them be exceeding hot fiery whoresons, and resolute as Hector, and as valiant as Troilus; then come off and on bravely, and lie by it, and sweat for't too, upon a good and a military advantage.

Enter FONTINELL.

CAMILLO
Prithee, have done; here comes the prisoner.

VIOLETTA
My lord Camillo, is this the gentleman
Whose valour by your valour is subdu'd?

CAMILLO
It is, fair lady, and I yield him up
To be your beauty's worthy prisoner.
Lord Fontinell, think your captivity
Happy in this; she that hath conquered me
Receives my conquest as my love's fair fee.

VIOLETTA
Fair stranger, droop not, since the chance of wars
Brings to the soldier death, restraint, or scars.

FONTINELL
Lady, I know the fortune of the field
Is death with honour, or with shame to yield,
As I have done.

VIOLETTA
In that no scandal lies;
Who dies when he may live, he doubly dies.

FONTINELL
My reputation's lost.

VIOLETTA
Nay, that's not so;
You fled not, but were vanquish'd by your foe.
The eye of war respects not you nor him;
It is our fate will have us lose or win.
You will disdain if I you prisoner call?

FONTINELL
No, but rejoice since I am beauty's thrall.

HIPOLITO
Enough of this; come, wenches, shake your heels.

CAMILLO
Music, advance thee on thy golden wing,
And dance division from sweet string to string.

FONTINELL
Camillo, I shall curb thy tyranny
In making me that lady's prisoner.
She has an angel's body, but within't,
Her coy heart says there lies a heart of flint.

Music for a measure. Whilst FONTINELL speaks, they dance a strain.

Such beauty be my jailor? A heavenly hell!
The darkest dungeon which spite can devise
To throw this carcass in, her glorious eyes
Can make as lightsome as the fairest chamber
In Paris Louvre. Come, captivity,
And chain me to her looks; how am I toss'd,
Being twice in mind, as twice in body lost!

VIOLETTA on a sudden breaks off, the rest stand talking.

CAMILLO
Not the measure out, fair mistress?

VIOLETTA
No, fair servant, not the measure out; I have on the sudden a foolish desire to be out of the measure.

CAMILLO
What breeds that desire?

VIOLETTA
Nay, I hope it is no breeding matter. Tush, tush, by my maidenhead, I will not; the music likes me not, and I have a shoe wrings me to th' heart. Besides, I have a woman's reason: I will not dance, because I will not dance. Prithee, dear Hero, take my prisoner there into the measure; fie, I cannot abide to see a man sad nor idle. I'll be out once, as the music is in mine ear.

FONTINELL
Lady, bid him whose heart no sorrow feels
Tickle the rushes with his wanton heels;
I have too much lead at mine.

FIRST LADY
I'll make it light.

FONTINELL
How?

FIRST LADY
By a nimble dance.

FONTINELL
You hit it right.

FIRST LADY
Your keeper bids you dance.

FONTINELL
Then I obey;
My heart I feel grows light, it melts away.

They dance, Violetta stands by marking Fontinell.

VIOLETTA
In troth, a very pretty Frenchman: the carriage of his body likes me well; so does his footing; so does his face; so does his eye above his face; so does himself, above all that can be above himself.
Camillo, thou hast played a foolish part;
Thy prisoner makes a slave of thy love's heart.
Shall Camillo then sing, "Willow, willow, willow?" Not for the world. No, no, my French prisoner; I will use thee Cupid knows how, and teach thee to fall into the hands of a woman. If I do not feed thee with fair looks, ne'er let me live; if thou getst out of my fingers till I have thy very heart, ne'er let me love. Nothing but thy life shall serve my turn, and how otherwise I'll plague thee, monsieur, you and I'll deal; only this because I'll be sure he shall not start, I'll lock him in a little low room besides himself, where his wanton eye shall see neither sun nor moon. So, the dance is done, and my heart has done her worst: made me in love. Farewell, my lord, I have much haste, you have many thanks; I am angered a little, but

am greatly pleas'd. If you wonder that I take this strange leave, excuse it thus, that women are strange fools and will take anything.

Exit.

HIPOLITO
Tricks, tricks, kerry merry buff! How now, lad, in a trance?

CAMILLO
Strange farewell. After, dear Hipolito.
O, what a maze is love of joy and woe!

Exeunt CAMILLO and HIPOLITO.

FONTINELL
Strange frenzy. After, wretched Fontinell.
Oh, what a heaven is love! Oh, what a hell!

Exit. Then exeunt omnes.

SCENE II. A Street Before Blurt's House

Enter LAZARILLO melancholy, and PILCHER his boy.

LAZARILLO
Boy, I am melancholy because I burn.

PILCHER
And I am melancholy because I am a-cold.

LAZARILLO
I pine away with the desire of flesh.

PILCHER
It's neither flesh nor fish that I pine for, but for both.

LAZARILLO
Pilcher, Cupid hath got me a stomach, and I long for lac'd mutton.

PILCHER
Plain mutton without a lace would serve me.

LAZARILLO
For as your tame monkey is your only best, and most only beast to your Spanish lady, or as your tobacco is your only smoker away of rheum and all other rheumatic diseases, or as your Irish louse does bite most naturally fourteen weeks after the change of your saffron-seamed shirt, or as the commodities

which are sent out of the Low Countries and put in vessels called Mother Cornelius' dry-fats are most common in France, so it pleaseth the destinies that I should thirst to drink out of a most sweet Italian vessel, being a Spaniard.

PILCHER
What vessel is that, signior?

LAZARILLO
A woman, Pilcher, the moist-handed Madonna Imperia, a most rare and divine creature.

PILCHER
A most rascally damn'd courtesan.

LAZARILLO
Boy, hast thou foraged the country for a new lodging? For I have sworn to lay my bones in this chitty of Venice.

PILCHER
Any man that sees us will swear that we shall both lay our bones, and nothing but bones, and we stalk here longer. They tell me, signior, I must go to the constable, and he is to see you lodg'd.

LAZARILLO
Inquire for that busy member of the chitty.

Enter DOYT and DANDIPRAT passing over the stage.

PILCHER
I will, and here come a leash of informers. Save you, plump youths.

DANDIPRAT
And thee, my lean stripling.

PILCHER
Which is the constable's house?

DOYT
That at the sign of the Brown Bill.

PILCHER
Farewell.

DANDIPRAT
Why, and farewell. [To DOYT] The rogue's made of pie crust, he's so short.

PILCHER
The officious gentleman inherits here.

LAZARILLO

Knock, or enter, and let thy voice pull him out by the ears.

He knocks.

DOYT
'Slid, Dandiprat, this is the Spanish curtal that in the last battle fled twenty miles ere he look'd behind him.

DANDIPRAT
Doyt, he did the wiser; but, sirrah, this block shall be a rare threshold for us to whet our wits upon. Come, let's about our business, and if here we find him at our return, he shall find us this month in knavery.

Exeunt DOYT and DANDIPRAT.

PILCHER
What ho! Nobody speaks. Where dwells the constable?

Enter BLURT and SLUBBER the beadle.

BLURT
Here dwells the constable. [To SLUBBER] Call assistance, give them my full charge, raise if you see cause. [To PILCHER] Now, sir, what are you, sir?

PILCHER
Follower to that Spanish-leather gentleman.

BLURT
And what are you, sir, that cry out upon me? [To SLUBBER] Look to his tools. [To LAZARILLO] What are you, sir? Speak, what are you? I charge you, what are you?

LAZARILLO
Most clear mirror of magistrates, I am servitor to god Mars.

BLURT
For your serving of God I am not to meddle. Why do you raise me?

LAZARILLO
I desire to have a wide room in your favour: sweet blood, cast away your name upon me, for I neither know you by your face, nor by your voice.

BLURT
It may be so, sir. I have two voices in any company: one, as I am master constable; another, as I am Blurt; and the third, as I am Blurt, master constable.

LAZARILLO
I understand, you are a mighty pillar or post in the chitty.

BLURT
I am a poor post, but not to stand at every man's door, without my bench of bill-men. I am, for a better, the duke's own image, and charge you in his name to obey me.

LAZARILLO
I do so.

BLURT
I am to stand, sir, in any bawdy house, or sink of wickedness. I am the duke's own grace, and in any fray or resurrection, am to bestir my stumps as well as he. I charge you know this staff.

SLUBBER
Turn the arms to him.

BLURT
Upon this may I lean, and no man say black's mine eye.

LAZARILLO
Whosoever says you have a black eye is a camooche. Most great Blurt, I do unpent-house the roof of my carcass and touch the knee of thy office in Spanish compliment. I desire to sojourn in your chitty.

BLURT
Sir, sir, for fault of a better, I am to charge you not to keep a-soldiering in our city without a precept. Besides, by my office I am to search and examine you. Have you the duke's hand to pass?

LAZARILLO
Signior, no, I have the general's hand at large, and all his fingers.

BLURT
Except it be for the general good of the commonwealth, the general cannot lead you up and down our city.

LAZARILLO
I have the general's hand to pass through the world at my pleasure.

BLURT
At your pleasure! That's rare. Then, roly-poly, our wives shall lie at your command. Your general has no such authority in my precinct, and therefore I charge you pass no further.

LAZARILLO
I tell thee, I will pass through the world, thou little morsel of justice, and eat twenty such as thou art.

BLURT
Sir, sir, you shall find Venice out of the world: I'll tickle you for that.

LAZARILLO
I will pass through the world, as Alexander Magnus did, to conquer.

BLURT
As Alexander of Saint Magnus did? That's another matter: you might have informed this at the first, and you never needed to have come to your answer. Let me see your pass; if it be not the duke's hand, I'll tickle you for all this. Quickly, I pray; this staff is to walk in other places.

LAZARILLO
There it is.

BLURT
Slubber, read it over.

LAZARILLO
Read it yourself; what besonian is that?

BLURT
This is my clerk, sir; he has been clerk to a good many bonds and bills of mine. I keep him only to read, for I cannot; my office will not let me.

PILCHER
Why do you put on your spectacles then?

BLURT
To see that he read right. How now, Slubber, is't the duke's hand? I'll tickle him else.

SLUBBER
Mass, 'tis not like his hand.

BLURT
Look well; the duke has a wart on the back of his hand.

SLUBBER
Here's none, on my word, master constable, but a little blot.

BLURT
Blot? Let's see, let's see. Ho, that stands for the wart; do you not see the trick of that? Stay, stay; is there not a little prick in the hand? for the duke's hand had a prick in't when I was with him, with opening oysters.

SLUBBER
Yes, mass, here's one; besides, 'tis a goodly great long hand.

BLURT
So has the duke a goodly huge hand; I have shook him by it (God forgive me) ten thousand times. He must pass like Alexander of Saint Magnus. Well, sir,—'tis your duty to stand bare—the duke has sent his fist to me, and I were a Jew if I should shrink for it. I obey; you must pass, but pray take heed with what dice you pass, I mean what company, for Satan is most busy where he finds one like himself. Your name, sir?

LAZARILLO
Lazarillo de Tormes in Castille, cousin-german to the adolantado of Spain.

BLURT
Are you so, sir? God's blessing on your heart. Your name again, sir, if it be not too tedious for you?

LAZARILLO
Lazarillo de Tormes in Castille, cousin-german to the Spanish adolantado.

SLUBBER
I warrant he's a great man in his own country.

BLURT
H'as a good name; Slubber, set it down: write, Lazarus in torment at the castle, and a cozening German at the sign of the Falantido diddle in Spain. So, sir, you are engross'd. You must give my officer a groat; it's nothing to me, signior.

LAZARILLO
I will cancel when it comes to a sum.

BLURT
Well, sir, well; he shall give you an item for't. [To SLUBBER] Make a bill and he'll tear it, he says.

LAZARILLO
Most admirable Blurt, I am a man of war and profess fighting.

BLURT
I charge you, in the duke's name, keep the peace.

LAZARILLO
By your sweet favour, most dear Blurt, you charge too fast; I am a hanger-on upon Mars, and have a few crowns.

PILCHER
Two, his own and mine.

LAZARILLO
And desire you to point out a fair lodging for me and my train.

BLURT
'Tis my office, signior, to take men up a-nights; but if you will, my maids shall take you up a-mornings, since you profess fighting. I will commit you, signior, to mine own house; but will you pitch and pay, or will your worship run—

LAZARILLO
I scorn to run from the face of Thamer Cham.

BLURT

Then, sir, you mean not to run?

LAZARILLO
Signior, no.

BLURT
Bear witness, Slubber, that his answer is, Signior No: so now if he runs upon the score, I have him straight upon Signior No. This is my house, signior; enter.

LAZARILLO
March, excellent Blurt. Attend, Pilcher.

Exeunt LAZARILLO, BLURT, and SLUBBER.

Enter DOYT and DANDIPRAT.

PILCHER
Upon your trencher, signior, most hungerly.

DOYT
Now, sirrah, where's thy master?

PILCHER
The constable has press'd him.

DOYT
What, for a soldier?

PILCHER
Ay, for a soldier; but ere he'll go, I think, indeed, he and I shall press the constable.

DANDIPRAT
No matter; squeeze him, and leave no more liquor in him than in a dry'd neat's tongue. Sirrah Thin-gut, what's thy name?

PILCHER
My name, you chops? Why, I am of the blood of the Pilchers.

DANDIPRAT
Nay, 'sfoot, if one should kill thee, he could not be hang'd for't, for he would shed no blood; there's none in thee. Pilcher? Th'art a most pitiful dried one.

DOYT
I wonder thy master does not slice thee, and swallow thee for an anchovies.

PILCHER
He wants wine, boy, to swallow me down, for he wants money to swallow down wine. But farewell; I must dog my master.

DANDIPRAT
As long as thou dog'st a Spaniard, thou'lt ne'er be fatter. But stay; our haste is as great as thine, yet to endear ourselves into thy lean acquaintance, cry, rivo ho!, laugh and be fat, and for joy that we are met, we'll meet and be merry. Sing.

PILCHER
I'll make a shift to squeak.

DOYT
And I.

DANDIPRAT
And I, for my profession is to shift as well as you. Hem.

Sing. Music.

DOYT: What meat eats the Spaniard?
PILCHER: Dry'd pilchers and poor-john.
DANDIPRAT: Alas, thou art almost marr'd.
PILCHER: My cheeks are fall'n and gone.
DOYT: Would thou not leap at a piece of meat?
PILCHER: O, how my teeth do water; I could eat!
'Fore the heavens, my flesh is almost gone
With eating of pilcher and poor-john.

Exeunt.

ACT II

SCENE I. Outside A Tennis Court

Enter FONTINELL from tennis, and TRUEPENNY with him.

FONTINELL
Am I so happy then?

TRUEPENNY
Nay, sweet monsieur.

FONTINELL
O boy, thou hast new-wing'd my captiv'd soul!
Now to my fortune all the Fates may yield,
For I have won where first I lost the field.

TRUEPENNY

Why, sir, did my mistress prick you with the Spanish needle of her love, before I summon'd you from her to this parley?

FONTINELL
Doubts thou that, boy?

TRUEPENNY
Of mine honesty, I doubt extremely, for I cannot see the little god's tokens upon you. There is as much difference between you and a lover as between a cuckold and a unicorn.

FONTINELL
Why, boy?

TRUEPENNY
For you do not wear a pair of ruffled, frowning, ungartered stockings, like a gallant that hides his small-timber'd legs with a quail-pipe boot. Your hose stands upon too many points, and are not troubled with that falling sickness which follows pale, meagre, miserable, melancholy lovers. Your hands are not groping continually.

FONTINELL
Where, my little observer?

TRUEPENNY
In your greasy pocket, sir, like one that wants a cloak for the rain, and yet is still weather-beaten. Your hat nor head are not of the true heigh-ho block, for it should be broad-brimm'd, limber, like the skin of a white pudding when the meat is out, the facing fatty, the felt dusty, and not enter'd into any band; but your hat is of the nature of a loose, light, heavy-swelling wench, too strait-laced. I tell you, Monsieur, a lover should be all loose from the sole of the foot rising upward, and from the bases or confines of the slop falling downwards. If you were in my mistress's chamber, you should find othergates privy signs of love hanging out there.

FONTINELL
Have your little eyes watch'd so narrowly?

TRUEPENNY
Oh sir, a page must have a cat's eye, a spaniel's leg, a whore's tongue (a little tasting of the cog), a catchpole's hand (what he grips is his own), and a little, little body.

FONTINELL
Fair Violetta, I will wear thy love,
Like this French order, near unto my heart.
Via for fate! Fortune, lo, this is all.
At grief's rebound I'll mount, although I fall.

Enter CAMILLO and HIPOLITO from tennis, DOYT and DANDIPRAT with their cloaks and rapiers.

CAMILLO
Now, by Saint Mark, he's a most treacherous villain.

Dare the base Frenchman's eye gaze on my love?

HIPOLITO
Nay, sweet rogue, why wouldst thou make his face a vizard, to have two loopholes only? When he comes to a good face, may he not do with his eyes what he will? 'Sfoot, if I were as he, I'd pull them out, and if I wist they would anger thee.

CAMILLO
Thou add'st heat to my rage; away, stand back.
Dishonored slave, more treacherous than base,
This is the instance of my scorn'd disgrace.

FONTINELL
Thou ill-advis'd Italian, whence proceeds
This sudden fury?

CAMILLO
Villain, from thee.

HIPOLITO
Hercules
Stand between them!

FONTINELL
Villain? By my blood!
I am as free-born as your Venice duke!
Villain? Saint Dennis and my life to boot,
Thy lips shall kiss this pavement or my foot.

HIPOLITO
Your foot? With a pox! I hope y'are no pope, sir. His lips shall kiss my sister's soft lip, and thine, the tough lip of this. Nay, sir, I do but shew you that I have a tool. Do you hear, Saint Dennis? But that we both stand upon the narrow bridge of honour, I should cut your throat now, for pure love you bear to my sister, but that I know you would set out a throat.

CAMILLO
Wilt thou not stab the peasant
That thus dishonors both thyself and me?

HIPOLITO
Saint Mark set his marks upon me then. Stab? I'll have my shins broken, ere I'll scratch so much as the skin off a' the law of arms. Shall I make a Frenchman cry O! before the fall of the leaf? Not I, by the cross of this Dandiprat.

DANDIPRAT
If you will, sir, you shall coin me into a shilling.

HIPOLITO

I shall lay too heavy a cross upon thee then.

CAMILLO
Is this a time to jest? Boy, call my servants.

DOYT
Gentlemen, to the dresser!

Enter serving-men.

CAMILLO
You rogue, what dresser? Seize on Fontinell,
And lodge him in a dungeon presently.

FONTINELL
He steps upon his death that stirs a foot.

CAMILLO
That shall I try; as in the field before
I made thee stoop, so here I'll make thee bow.

FONTINELL
Thou played'st the soldier then, the villain now.

CAMILLO and his men set upon him, get him down and disweapon him, and hold him fast.

FONTINELL
Treacherous Italians!

CAMILLO
Hale him to a dungeon.
There, if your thoughts can apprehend the form
Of Violetta, dote on her rare feature;
Or if your proud flesh with a sparing diet
Can still retain her swelling spritefulness,
Then court instead of her the croaking vermin
That people that most solitary vault.

HIPOLITO
But sirrah Camillo, wilt thou play the wise and venerable bearded master constable and commit him indeed, because he would be meddling in thy precinct, and will not put off the cap of his love to the brown bill of thy desires? Well, thou hast given the law of arms a broken pate already; therefore, if thou wilt needs turn broker and be a cutthroat too, do. For my part, I'll go get a sweetball and wash my hands of it.

CAMILLO
Away with him; my life shall answer it.

FONTINELL
To prison must I then? Well, I will go,
And with a light-wing'd spirit insult o'er woe,
For in the darkest hell on earth, I'll find
Her fair idea to content my mind.
Yet France and Italy with blistered tongue
Shall publish thy dishonour in my wrong.
Oh, now how happy wert thou, couldst thou lodge me
Where I could leave to love her?

CAMILLO
By heaven I can.

FONTINELL
Thou canst? O happy man!
This is a kind of new invented law:
First feed the axe, after produce the saw.
Her heart no doubt will thy affections feel,
For thou'lt plead sighs in blood, and tears in steel.
Boy, tell my love her love thus sighing spake:
I'll vail my crest to death, for her dear sake.

Exit FONTINELL, guarded by serving-men.

CAMILLO
Boy? What boy is that?

HIPOLITO
Is't you, Sir Pandarus, the broking knight of Troy? Are your two legs the pair of trestles for the Frenchman to get up upon my sister?

TRUEPENNY
By the Nine Worthies, worthy gallants, not I. I, a gentleman for convenience? I, Sir Pandarus? Would Troy then were in my breeches, and I burnt worse than poor Troy. Sweet signior, you know, I know, and all Venice knows that my mistress scorns double-dealing with her heels.

HIPOLITO
With her heels? O, here's a sure pocket dag, and my sister shoots him off snipsnap at her pleasure. Sirrah Mephostophiles, did not you bring letters from my sister to the Frenchman?

TRUEPENNY
Signior, no.

CAMILLO
Did not you fetch him out of the tennis court?

TRUEPENNY
No, point, per ma foy. You see I have many tongues speak for me.

HIPOLITO
Did not he follow your crackship, at a beck given?

TRUEPENNY
Ita, true, certes, he spied, and I spitting thus, went thus.

HIPOLITO
But were stay'd thus.

TRUEPENNY
You hold a' my side, and therefore I must needs stick to you. 'Tis true; I going, he followed, and following, finger'd me, just as your worship does now. But I struggled and straggled, and wriggled and wraggled, and at last cried vale, valete, as I do now, with this fragment of rhyme:
My lady is grossly fall'n in love, and yet her waist is slender;
Had I not slipp'd away, you would have made my buttocks tender.

Exit.

DANDIPRAT
Shall Doyt and I play the bloodhounds and after him?

CAMILLO
No, let him run.

HIPOLITO
Not for this wager of my sister's love; run. Away, Dandiprat; catch Truepenny and hold him. Thyself shall pass more currant.

DANDIPRAT
I fly, sir; your Dandiprat is as light as a clipp'd angel.

Exit.

HIPOLITO
Nay, God's lid, after him, Camillo. Reply not, but away.

CAMILLO
Content; you know where to meet.

Exit.

HIPOLITO
For I know that the only way to win a wench is not to woo her; the only way to have her fast is to have her loose. The only way to triumph over her is to make her fall; and the way to make her fall—

DOYT
Is to throw her down.

HIPOLITO
Are you so cunning, sir?

DOYT
O Lord, sir, and have so perfit a master.

HIPOLITO
Well, sir, you know the gentlewoman that dwells in the midst of Saint Mark's Street.

DOYT
Midst of Saint Mark's Street, sir?

HIPOLITO
A pox on you! The flea-bitten-fac'd lady.

DOYT
Oh, sir, the freckle-cheek Madonna; I know her, signior, as well—

HIPOLITO
Not as I do, I hope, sir.

DOYT
No, sir, I'd be loath to have such inward acquaintance with her as you have.

HIPOLITO
Well, sir, slip, go presently to her, and from me deliver to her own white hands Fontinell's picture.

DOYT
Indeed, sir, she loves to have her chamber hung with the pictures of men.

HIPOLITO
She does. I'll keep my sister's eyes and his painted face asunder. Tell her besides, the masque holds and this the night, and nine the hour. Say we are all for her; away.

DOYT
And she's for you all, were you an army.

Exeunt.

SCENE II. A Room in Imperia's House

Enter IMPERIA the courtesan, two maids TRIVIA and SIMPERINA, with perfumes.

IMPERIA

Fie, fie, fie, fie, by the light oath of my fan, the weather is exceeding tedious and faint. Trivia, Simperina, stir, stir, stir; one of you open the casements, t'other take a ventoy and gently cool my face. Fie, I ha' such an exceeding high colour, I so sweat. Simperina, dost hear? Prithee be more compendious. Why, Simperina!

SIMPERINA
Here, madame.

IMPERIA
Press down my ruff before. Away; fie, how thou blow'st upon me. Thy breath, God's me, thy breath! Fie, fie, fie, fie, it takes off all the painting and colour from my cheek. In good faith, I care not if I go and be sick presently. Heigh ho, my head so aches with carrying this bodkin; in troth, I'll try if I can be sick.

TRIVIA
Nay, good sweet lady.

SIMPERINA
You know a company of gallants will be here at night; be not out of temper, sweet mistress.

IMPERIA
In good troth, if I be not sick I must be melancholy then. This same gown never comes on but I am so melancholy, and so sun-burnt: 'tis a strange garment. I warrant, Simperina, the foolish tailor that made it was troubled with the stitch when he composed it.

SIMPERINA
That's very likely, madame, but it makes you have, oh, a most incony body.

IMPERIA
No, no, no, no, by Saint Mark, the waist is not long enough, for I love a long and tedious waist. Besides, I have a most ungodly middle in it, and fie, fie, fie, fie, it makes me bend i' th' back. Oh, let me have some music.

Music.

SIMPERINA
That's not the fault in your gown, madame, but of your body.

IMPERIA
Fa la la, fa la la—indeed, the bending of the back is the fault of the body—la la la la, fa la la, fa la la, la la lah.

TRIVIA
O rich!

SIMPERINA
O rare!

IMPERIA

No, no, no, no, no; 'tis slight and common all that I do. Prithee, Simperina, do not ingle me; do not flatter me, Trivia. I ha' never a cast gown till the next week. Fa la la, la la la, fa la la, fa la la, etc. This stirring to and fro has done me much good. A song, I prithee; I love these French movings. Oh, they are so clean; if you tread them true, you shall hit them to a hair. Sing, sing, sing some odd and fantastical thing, for I cannot abide these dull and lumpish tunes. The musician stands longer a-pricking them than I would do to hear them. No, no, no, give me your light ones that go nimbly and quick, and are full of changes and carry sweet division. Ho, prithee sing. Stay, stay, stay; here's Hipolito's sonnet. First read it and then sing it.

Reads. Song.

SIMPERINA: In a fair woman what thing is best?
TRIVIA: I think a coral lip.
SIMPERINA: No, no, you jest;
She has a better thing.
TRIVIA: Then 'tis a pretty eye.
SIMPERINA: Yet 'tis a better thing,
Which more delight does bring.
TRIVIA: Then 'tis a cherry cheek.
SIMPERINA: No, no, you lie.
Were neither lip, nor cheeks coral, nor pretty eyes,
Were not her swelling breast stuck with strawberries,
Nor had smooth hand, soft skin, white neck, pure eye,
Yet she at this alone your love can tie:
It is, O 'tis the only joy to men,
The only praise to women. What is't then?
This it is, O, this it is, and in a woman's middle it is plac'd,
In a most beauteous body, a heart most chaste:
This is the jewel kings may buy;
If women sell this jewel, women lie.

One knocks within, Frisco answers within.

FRISCO
[Within] Who the pox knocks?

DOYT
[Within] One that will knock thy coxcomb if he do not enter.

FRISCO
[Within] If thou dost not enter, how canst thou knock me?

DOYT
[Within] Why then I'll knock thee when I do enter.

FRISCO
[Within] Why then thou shalt not enter, but instead of me knock thy heels.

DOYT
[Within] Frisco, I am Doyt, Hipolito's page.

FRISCO
[Within] And I am Frisco, squire to a bawdy house.

DOYT
[Within] I have a jewel to deliver to thy mistress.

FRISCO
[Within] Is't set with precious stones?

DOYT
[Within] Thick, thick, thick.

Enter DOYT with the picture, and FRISCO.

FRISCO
Why, enter then, thick, thick, thick.

IMPERIA
Fie, fie, fie, fie, fie; who makes that yawling at door?

FRISCO
Here's Signior Hipolito's man (that shall be) come to hang you.

IMPERIA
Trivia, strip that villain; Simperina, pinch him, slit his wide nose. Fie, fie, fie, I'll have you gelded for this lustiness.

FRISCO
And she threatens to geld me unless I be lusty, what shall poor Frisco do?

IMPERIA
Hang me.

FRISCO
Not I; hang me if you will, and set up my quarters too.

IMPERIA
Hipolito's boy come to hang me?

DOYT
To hang you with jewels, sweet and gentle; that's Frisco's meaning, and that's my coming.

IMPERIA
Keep the door.

FRISCO
That's my office indeed. I have been your doorkeeper for so long, that all the hinges, the spring-locks and the ring are worn to pieces. How if anybody knock at the door?

IMPERIA
Let them enter.

[Exit FRISCO.]

Fie, fie, fie, fie, fie, his great tongue does so run through my little ears; 'tis more harsh than a younger brother's courting of a gentlewoman, when he has no crowns. Boy?

DOYT
At your service.

IMPERIA
My service? Alas, alas, thou canst do me small service. Did thy master send this painted gentleman to me?

DOYT
This painted gentleman to you.

IMPERIA
Well, I will hang his picture up by the walls till I see his face, and when I see his face, I'll take his picture down. Hold it, Trivia.

TRIVIA
It's most sweetly made.

IMPERIA
Hang him up, Simperina.

SIMPERINA
It's a most sweet man.

IMPERIA
And does the masque hold? [To SIMPERINA] Let me see it again.

DOYT
If their vizards hold, here you shall see all their blind cheeks; this is the night, nine the hour, and I the jack that gives warning.

SIMPERINA
He gives warning, mistress; shall I let him out?

DOYT
You shall not need; I can set out myself.

Exit.

IMPERIA
Flaxen hair, and short too; oh, that's the French cut. But fie, fie, fie, these flaxen-hair'd men are such pulers, and such piddlers, and such chicken-hearts—and yet great quarrellers—that when they court a lady, they are for the better part bound to the peace. No, no, no, no, your black-haired man, so he be fair, is your only sweet man, and in any service, the most active. A banquet, Trivia; quick, quick, quick, quick, quick.

TRIVIA
In a twinkling. [Aside] 'Slid, my mistress cries like the rod-woman: "Quick, quick, quick, buy any rosemary and bays?"

Exit.

IMPERIA
A little face, but a lovely face; fie, fie, fie, no matter what face he make, so the other parts be legitimate and go upright. Stir, stir, Simperina. Be doing, be doing, quickly; move, move, move.

SIMPERINA
Most incontinently. [Aside] Move, move, move. O sweet!

Exit.

IMPERIA
Heigh ho! As I live, I must love thee and suck kisses from thy lips; alack, that women should fall thus deeply in love with dumb things that have no feeling. But they are women's crosses, and the only way to take them is to take them patiently.

Enter FRISCO, TRIVIA and SIMPERINA.

Heigh ho! Set music, Frisco.

FRISCO
Music, if thou hast not a hard heart, speak to my mistress.

[Music.]

IMPERIA
Say he scorn to marry me, yet he shall stand me in some stead by being my Ganymede. If he be the most decayed gallant in all Venice, I will myself undo myself and my whole state to set him up again. Though speaking truth would save my life, I will lie to do him pleasure; yet to tell lies may hurt the soul. Fie, no, no, no; souls are things to be trodden under our feet, when we dance after love's pipe. Therefore, here, hang this counterfeit at my bed's feet.

FRISCO
If he be counterfeit, nail him up upon one of your posts.

Exit with picture.

IMPERIA
By the moist hand of love, I swear I will be his lottery, and he shall never draw but it shall be a prize.

CURVETTO knock within.

FRISCO
[Within] Who knocks?

CURVETTO
[Within] Why, 'tis I, knave.

FRISCO
[Within] Then, knave, knock there still.

CURVETTO
[Within] Wut open door?

FRISCO
[Within] Yes, when I list I will.

CURVETTO
[Within] Here's money.

FRISCO
[Within] Much!

CURVETTO
[Within] Here's gold.

FRISCO
[Within] Away!

CURVETTO
[Within] Knave, open!

FRISCO
[Within] Call to our maids, "Good night": we are all a-slopen.

[Enters.

Mistress, if you have ever a pinnace to set out, you may now have it mann'd and rigg'd, for Signior Curvetto, he that cries, "I am an old courtier, but lie close, lie close," when our maids swear he lies as wide as any courtier in Italy—

IMPERIA
Do we care how he lies?

Knocking.

FRISCO
Anon, anon, anon. This old hoary red deer serves himself in at your keyhole.

CURVETTO
[Within] What, Frisco?

FRISCO
Hark, shall he enter the breach?

IMPERIA
Fie, fie, fie. I wonder what this gurnet's head makes here. Yet bring him in; he will serve for picking meat. [Exit FRISCO.] Let music play, for I will feign myself to be asleep.

Enter FRISCO with CURVETTO.

CURVETTO
Three pence, and here's a teston. Yet take all;
Coming to jump we must be prodigal.
Hem!
I am an old courtier, and I can lie close;
Put up, Frisco, put up, put up, put up.

FRISCO
Anything at your hands, sir, I will put up, because you seldom pull out anything.

SIMPERINA
Softly, sweet Signior Curvetto, for she's fast.

CURVETTO
Ha, fast? My roba fast? and but young night?
She's wearied, wearied; ah ha, hit I right?

SIMPERINA
How, sir, wearied? Marry, foh!

FRISCO
Wearied, sir? Marry muff!

CURVETTO
No words? Here, mouse, no words, no words? Sweet rose,
I am an hoary courtier, and lie close, lie close.
Hem!

FRISCO

An old hoary courtier? Why, so has a jowl of ling and a musty whiting been, time out of mind. Methinks, signior, you should not be so old by your face.

CURVETTO
I have a good heart, knave, and a good heart
Is a good face-maker. I am young, quick, brisk.
I was a reveller in a long stock;
There's not a gallant now fills such a stock:
Plump hose, pan'd, stuff'd with hair (hair then was held
The lightest stuffing); a fair codpiece, hoh;
An eel-skin sleeve, lash'd here and there with lace;
High collar, lash'd again; breech lash'd also;
A little simp'ring ruff; a dapper cloak
With Spanish-button'd cape; my rapier here,
Gloves like a burgomaster here, hat here,
Stuck with some ten-groat brooch; and over all
A goodly, long, thick, Abram-color'd beard.
Ho God, ho God! thus did I revel it,
When Monsieur Motte lay here ambassador.
But now those beards are gone, our chins are bare;
Our courters now do all against the hair.
I can lie close and see this, but not see;
I am hoary, but not hoary as some be.

IMPERIA
Heigh ho! Who's that? Signior Curvetto? By my virginity—

CURVETTO
Hem, no more.
Swear not so deep at these years: men have eyes,
And though the most are fools, some fools are wise.

IMPERIA
Fie, fie, fie; and you meet me thus at half-weapon, one must down.

FRISCO
[Aside] She for my life.

IMPERIA
Somebody shall pay for't.

FRISCO
[Aside] He for my head.

IMPERIA
Do not therefore come over me so with cross blows. No, no, no, I shall be sick if my speech be stopp'd. By my virginity I swear— and why may not I swear by that I have not, as well as poor musty soldiers do by their honour, brides and four and twenty (ha, ha, ha!) by their maidenheads, citizens by their faith,

and brokers as they hope to be saved?—by my virginity I swear, I dream'd that one brought me a goodly codshead, and in one of the eyes there stuck, methought, the greatest precious stone, the most sparkling diamond. Oh fie, fie, fie, fie, fie, that diamonds should make women such fools.

CURVETTO
A codshead and a diamond? Ha, ha, ha!
'Tis common, common; you may dream as well
Of diamonds and of codsheads, where's not one,
As swear by your virginity, where's none.
[Aside] I am that codshead; she has spied my stone,
My diamond. Noble wench, but nobler hose.

Puts it up.

I am an old courtier, and lie close, lie close.

The cornets sound a lavolta which the maskers are to dance. CAMILLO, HIPOLITO, and other gallants, everyone save HIPOLITO with a lady, mask'd, zanies with torches enter suddenly. CURVETTO offers to depart.

IMPERIA
No, no, no, if you shrink from me I will not love you; stay.

CURVETTO
I am conjur'd, and will keep my circle.

They dance.

IMPERIA
Fie, fie, fie, by the neat tongue of eloquence, this measure is out of measure; 'tis too hot, too hot. Gallants, be not ashamed to show your own faces. Ladies, unapparel your dear beauties. So, so, so, so, here is a banquet; sit, sit, sit. Signior Curvetto, thrust in among them. Soft music there! do, do, do.

CURVETTO
I will first salute the men, close with the women, and last sit.

HIPOLITO
But not sit last: a banquet! and have these suckets here! Oh, I have a crew of angels prisoners in my pocket, and none but a good bale of dice can fetch them out. Dice, ho! Come, my little lecherous baboon; by Saint Mark, you shall venture your twenty crowns.

CURVETTO
And have but one.

HIPOLITO
I swore first.

CURVETTO

Right, you swore,
[Aside] But oaths are now like Blurt our constable,
Standing for nothing, a mere plot, a trick.
The masque dogg'd me; I hit it in the nick:
A fetch to get my diamond, my dear stone.
I am a hoary courtier, but lie close, close, close.
[To HIPOLITO] I'll play, sir.

HIPOLITO
Come.

CURVETTO
But in my t'other hose.

Exit.

OMNES
Curvetto?

HIPOLITO
Let him go. I knew what hook would choke him, and therefore baited that for him to nibble upon; an old coxcomb rascal that was beaten out a' th' cock-pit, when I could not stand a' high lone without I held by a thing, to come crowing among us. Hang him, lobster! Come, the same oath that your foreman took, take all, and sing.

Song.
Love is like a lamb, and love is like a lion.
Fly from love, he fights; fight, then does he fly on.
Love is all in fire, and yet is ever freezing;
Love is much in winning, yet is more in leezing.
Love is ever sick, and yet is never dying;
Love is ever true, and yet is ever lying.
Love does dote in liking, and is mad in loathing;
Love indeed is anything, yet indeed is nothing.

Enter LAZARILLO.

LAZARILLO
Mars armipotent with his court of guard, give sharpness to my toledo; I am beleaguer'd! O Cupid grant that my blushing prove not a linstock, and give fire too suddenly to the Roaring Meg of my desires! Most sanguine-cheek'd ladies!

HIPOLITO
'Sfoot, how now, Don Dego? Sanguine-cheek'd? Dost think their faces have been at cutler's? Out, you roaring tawny-fac'd rascal! 'Twere a good deed to beat my hilts about's coxcomb, and then make him sanguine-cheek'd too.

CAMILLO

Nay, good Hipolito.

IMPERIA
Fie, fie, fie, fie, fie; tho' I hate his company, I would not have my house to abuse his countenance. No, no, no, be not so contagious; I will send him hence with a flea in's ear.

HIPOLITO
Do, or I'll turn him into a flea and make him skip under some of your petticoats.

IMPERIA
Signior Lazarillo.

LAZARILLO
Most sweet face, you need not hang out your silken tongue as a flag of truce, for I will drop at your feet ere I draw blood in your chamber; yet I shall hardly drink up this wrong. For your sake, I will wipe it out for this time. I would deal with you in secret, so you had a void room, about most deep and serious matters.

IMPERIA
I'll send these hence. [Aside] Fie, fie, fie, I am so chok'd still with this man of gingerbread, and yet I can never be rid of him. But hark, Hipolito. [Whispers to HIPOLITO]

HIPOLITO
Good; draw the curtains, put out candles, and girls, to bed.

LAZARILLO
Venus, give me suck from thine own most white and tender dugs that I may batten in love. Dear instrument of many men's delight, are all these women?

IMPERIA
No, no, no; they are half men and half women.

LAZARILLO
You apprehend too fast. I mean by women, wives, for wives are no maids, nor are maids women. If those unbearded gallants keep the doors of their wedlock, those ladies spend their hours of pastime but ill, O most rich armful of beauty! But if you can bring all those females into one ring, into one private place, I will read a lecture of discipline to their most great and honourable ears, wherein I will teach them so to carry their white bodies, either before their husbands or before their lovers, that they shall never fear to have milk thrown in their faces, nor I wine in mine, when I come to sit upon them in courtesy.

IMPERIA
That were excellent; I'll have them all here at your pleasure.

LAZARILLO
I will show them all the tricks and garbs of Spanish dames; I will study for apt and elegant phrase to tickle them with. And when my devise is ready, I will come. Will you inspire into your most divine spirits the most divine soul of tobacco?

IMPERIA
No, no, no; fie, fie, fie. I should be chok'd up if your pipe should kiss my underlip.

LAZARILLO
Henceforth, most deep stamp of feminine perfection, my pipe shall not be drawn before you, but in secret.

Enter HIPOLITO and the rest of the masquers, as before, dancing. HIPOLITO takes IMPERIA.

Exeunt all but LAZARILLO.

LAZARILLO
Lament my case; since thou canst not provoke
Her nose to smell, love fill thine own with smoke.

Exit.

ACT III

SCENE I. A Street Before Hipolito's House

Enter HIPOLITO and FRISCO.

FRISCO
The wooden picture you sent her hath set her on fire, and she desires you, as you pity the case of a poor desperate gentlewoman, to serve that monsieur in at supper to her.

Enter CAMILLO.

HIPOLITO
The Frenchman! Saint Dennis, let her carve him up! Stay, here's Camillo. Now, my fool in fashion, my sage idiot, up with these brims, down with this devil Melancholy. Are you decayed, concupiscentious inamorato? News, news: Imperia dotes on Fontinell.

CAMILLO
What comfort speaks her love to my sick heart?

HIPOLITO
Marry, this, sir. Here's a yellow-hammer flew to me with thy water; and I cast it and find that his mistress, being given to this new falling-sickness, will cure thee. The Frenchman, you see, has a soft marmalady heart, and shall no sooner feel Imperia's liquorish desire to lick at him, but straight he'll stick the brooch of her longing in it. Then sir, may you, sir, come upon my sister, sir, with a fresh charge, sir. Sa, sa, sa, sa; once giving back, and thrice coming forward, she yield and the town of Brest is taken.

CAMILLO
This hath some taste of hope. Is that the Mercury

Who brings you notice of his mistress' love?

FRISCO
I may be her Mercury for my running of errands; but troth, sir, I am Cerebrus, for I am porter to hell.

CAMILLO
Then, Cerebrus, play thy part; here, search that hell,
There find and bring forth that false Fontinell.

Exit FRISCO.

If I can win his stray'd thoughts to retire
From her encountered eyes, whom I have singled
In Hymen's holy battle, he shall pass
From hence to France, in company and guard
Of mine own heart. He comes, Hipolito.

Enter FONTINELL talking with FRISCO.

Still looks he like a lover, poor gentleman.
Love is the mind's strong physic and the pill
That leaves the heart sick and o'erturns the will.

FONTINELL
O happy persecution, I embrace thee
With an unfettered soul. So sweet a thing
Is it to sigh upon the rack of love,
Where each calamity is groaning witness
Of the poor martyr's faith. I never heard
Of any true affection but 'twas nipp'd
With care, that like the caterpillar eats
The leaves off the spring's sweetest book, the rose.
"Love bred on earth is often nurs'd in hell;
By rote it reads woe, ere it learn to spell."

CAMILLO
Good morrow, French lord.

HIPOLITO
Bon jour, Monsieur.

FONTINELL
To your secure and more than happy self
I tender thanks, for you have honour'd me;
You are my jailor and have penn'd me up,
Lest the poor fly your prisoner should alight
Upon your mistress' lip, and thence derive
The dimpled print of an infective touch.

Thou secure tyrant, yet unhappy lover,
Couldst thou chain mountains to my captive feet,
Yet Violetta's heart and mine should meet.

HIPOLITO
Hark, swaggerer, there's a little dapple-colour'd rascal, ho, a bona roba. Her name's Imperia, a gentlewoman, by my faith, of an ancient house, and has goodly rents and comings in of her own; and this ape would fain have thee chain'd to her in the holy state. Sirrah, she's fall'n in love with thy picture; yes, faith. To her, woo her, and win her. Leave my sister and thy ransom's paid, all's paid, gentlemen. By th' Lord, Imperia is as good a girl as any is in Venice.

CAMILLO
Upon mine honour, Fontinell, 'tis true;
The lady dotes on thy perfections.
Therefore resign my Violetta's heart
To me, the lord of it, and I will send thee—

FONTINELL
O whither, to damnation? Wilt thou not?
Think'st thou the purity of my true soul
Can taste your leperous counsel? No, I defy you.
Incestancy dwell on his rivelled brow
That weds for dirt, or on th'enforced heart,
That lags in rearward of his father's charge
When to some negro-gelderling he's clogg'd
By the injunction of a golden fee.
When I call back my vows to Violetta,
May I then slip into an obscure grave,
Whose mould, unpress'd with stony monument,
Dwelling in open air, may drink the tears
Of the inconstant clouds to rot me soon
Out of my private linen sepulchre.

CAMILLO
Ay, is this your settled resolution?

FONTINELL
By my love's best divinity, it is.

CAMILLO
Then bear him to his prison back again;
This tune must alter ere thy lodging mend.
To death, fond Frenchman, thy slight love doth tend.

FONTINELL
Then, constant heart, thy fate with joy pursue;
Draw wonder to thy death, expiring true.

Exit.

HIPOLITO
After him, Frisco; enforce thy mistress's passion. Thou shalt have access to him to bring him love tokens. If they prevail not, yet thou shalt still be in presence, be't but to spite him. In, honest Frisco.

FRISCO
I'll vex him to the heart, sir, fear me not;
[Aside] Yet here's a trick perchance may set him free.

Exit.

HIPOLITO
Come, wilt thou go laugh and lie down? Now sure there be some rebels in thy belly, for thine eyes do nothing but watch and ward, tho' 'ast not slept these three nights.

CAMILLO
Alas, how can I? He that truly loves
Burns out the day in idle fantasies;
And when the lamb bleating doth bid good night
Unto the closing day, then tears begin
To keep quick time unto the owl, whose voice
Shrieks like the bellman in the lover's ears.
Love's eye the jewel of sleep, oh, seldom wears!
The early lark is wakened from her bed,
Being only by love's plaints disquieted,
And singing in the morning's ease, she weeps,
Being deep in love, at lovers' broken sleeps.
But say a golden slumber chance to tie
With silken strings the cover of love's eye;
Then dreams, magician-like, mocking present
Pleasures, whose fading leaves more discontent.
Have you these golden charms?

Enter Musicians.

OMNES
We have, my lord.

CAMILLO
Bestow them sweetly; think a lover's heart
Dwells in each instrument, and let it melt
In weeping strains. Yonder direct your faces,
That the soft summons of a frightless parley
May creep into the casement; so, begin.
Music, speak movingly; assume my part,
For thou must now plead to a stony heart.

Song.

Pity, pity, pity,
Pity, pity, pity:
That word begins that ends a true-love ditty.
Your blessed eyes, like a pair of suns,
Shine in the sphere of smiling.
Your pretty lips, like a pair of doves,
Are kisses still compiling.
Mercy hangs upon your brow, like a precious jewel;
O, let not then,
Most lovely maid, best to be loved of men,
Marble lie upon your heart, that will make you cruel.
Pity, pity, pity,
Pity, pity, pity:
That word begins that ends a true-love ditty.

VIOLETTA above.

VIOLETTA
Who owes this salutation?

CAMILLO
Thy Camillo.

VIOLETTA
Is not your shadow there too, my sweet brother?

HIPOLITO
Here, sweet sister.

VIOLETTA
I dreamt so. O, I am much bound to you,
For you, my lord, have us'd my love with honour.

CAMILLO
Ever with honour.

VIOLETTA
Indeed, indeed, you have.

HIPOLITO
'Slight, she means her French garsoon.

VIOLETTA
The same. Good night; trust me, 'tis somewhat late,
And this bleak wind nips dead all idle prate.
I must to bed, good night.

CAMILLO
The god of rest
Play music to thine eyes, whilst on my breast
The Furies sit and beat, and keep care waking.

HIPOLITO
You will not leave my friend in this poor taking.

VIOLETTA
Yes, by the velvet brow of darkness.

HIPOLITO
You scurvy tit; 'sfoot, scurvy anything! Do you hear, Susanna? You punk, if I geld not your muskcat! I'll do't, by Jesu! Let's go, Camillo.

VIOLETTA
Nay, but, pure swaggerer, ruffian, do you think
To fright me with your bugbear threats? Go by!
Hark, tosspot, in your ear: the Frenchman's mine,
And by these hands I'll have him.

HIPOLITO
Rare rogue! Fine!

VIOLETTA
He is my prisoner, by a deed of gift;
Therefore, Camillo, you have wrong'd me much
To wrong my prisoner. By my troth, I love him
The rather for the baseness he endures
For my unworthy self. I'll tell you what:
Release him, let him plead your love for you.
I love a' life to hear a man speak French
Of his complexion; I would undergo
The instruction of that language rather far
Than be two weeks unmarried, by my life.
Because I'll speak true French, I'll be his wife.

CAMILLO
O, scorn to my chaste love! Burst heart!

HIPOLITO
'Swounds, hold!

CAMILLO
Come, gentle friends, tie your most solemn tunes
By silver strings unto a leaden pace.
False fair, enjoy thy base-belov'd; adieu.

He's far less noble, and shall prove less true.

Exeunt all but VIOLETTA. Enter TRUEPENNY above with a letter.

TRUEPENNY
Lady, Imperia the courtesan's zany hath brought you this letter from the poor gentleman in the deep dungeon, but would not stay till he had an answer.

VIOLETTA
Her groom employed by Fontinell? O, strange!
I wonder how he got access to him.
I'll read, and reading, my poor heart shall ache:
"True love is jealous; fears the best love shake."
[Reading] "Meet me at the end of the old chapel, next Saint Lorenzo's monastery; furnish your company with a friar, that there he may consummate our holy vows. Till midnight, farewell.
Thine Fontinell."
Hath he got opportunity to 'scape?
O happy period of our separation!
Blest night, wrap Cynthia in a sable sheet,
That fearful lovers may securely meet!

[Exeunt.]

SCENE II. An Old Chapel

Enter FRISCO in Fontinell's apparel, FONTINELL making himself ready in Frisco's. They enter suddenly and in fear.

FRISCO
Play you my part bravely; you must look like a slave, and you shall see I'll counterfeit a Frenchman most knavishly. My mistress, for your sake, charg'd me on her blessing to fall to these shifts. I left her at cards; she'll sit up till you come because she'll have you play a game at noddy. You'll to her presently?

FONTINELL
I will, upon mine honour.

FRISCO
I think she does not greatly care whether you fall to her upon your honour or no. So, all's fit; tell my lady that I go in a suit of durance for her sake. That's your way, and this pithole's mine. If I can 'scape hence, why so; if not, he that's hang'd is nearer to heaven by half a score steps than he that dies in a bed, and so adieu, monsieur.

Exit.

FONTINELL
Farewell, dear trusty slave. Shall I profane

This temple with an idol of strange love?
When I do so, let me dissolve in fire.
Yet one day will I see this dame, whose heart
Takes off my misery. I'll not be so rude
To pay her kindness with ingratitude.

Enter VIOLETTA and a friar apace.

VIOLETTA
My dearest Fontinell!

FONTINELL
My Violetta!
Oh God!

VIOLETTA
Oh God!

FONTINELL
Where is this reverend friar?

FRIAR
Here, overjoy'd, young man.

VIOLETTA
How didst thou 'scape?
How came Imperia's man?

FONTINELL
No more of that.

VIOLETTA
When did Imperia—

FONTINELL
Questions now are thieves,
And lies in ambush to surprise our joys.
My most happy stars shine still, shine on.
Away, come; love beset had need be gone.

Exeunt.

SCENE III. A Room in Imperia's House

Enter CURVETTO and SIMPERINA.

CURVETTO
I must not stay, thou sayst?

SIMPERINA
Gods me, away!

CURVETTO
Buss, buss again. Here's sixpence; buss again.
Farewell, I must not stay then.

SIMPERINA
Foh.

CURVETTO
Farewell.
At ten a' clock thou sayst, and ring a bell
Which thou wilt hang out at this window?

SIMPERINA
Lord,
She'll hear this fiddling.

CURVETTO
No, close, on my word.
Farewell; just ten a' clock, I shall come in.
Remember to let down the cord. Just ten
Thou'lt open, mouse? Pray God thou dost; Amen! Amen! Amen!
I am an old courtier, wench, but I can spy
A young duck. Close, mum. Ten. Close, 'tis not I.

Exit CURVETTO.

SIMPERINA
Mistress! Sweet ladies!

Enter IMPERIA and courtesans, with tablebooks.

IMPERIA
Is his old rotten aqua-vitae bottle stopp'd up? Is he gone? Fie, fie, fie, fie, he so smells of ale and onions and rosa-solis, fie. Bolt the door, stop the keyhole, lest his breath peep in; burn some perfume. I do not love to handle these dry'd stockfishes that ask so much tawing, fie, fie, fie.

FIRST COURTESAN
Nor I, trust me, lady. Fie!

IMPERIA

No, no, no, no; stools and cushions, low stools, low stools. Sit, sit, sit round, ladies, round. So, so, so, so, let your sweet beauties be spread to the full and most moving advantage, for we are fall'n into his hands, who they say has an ABC for the sticking in of the least white pin in any part of the body.

SECOND COURTESAN
Madame Imperia, what stuff is he like to draw out before us?

IMPERIA
Nay, nay, nay, 'tis Greek to me, 'tis Greek to me. I never had remnant of his Spanish-leather learning. Here he comes; your cares may now fit themselves out of the whole piece.

Enter LAZARILLO.

LAZARILLO
I do first deliver to your most skreet and long-finger'd hands this head, or top of all the members, bare and uncomb'd, to show how deeply I stand in reverence of your naked female beauties. Bright and unclipp'd angels, if I were to make a discovery of any new-found land, as Virginia or so, to ladies and courtiers, my speech should hoist up sails fit to bear up such lofty and well-rigged vessels; but because I am to deal only with the civil chitty matron, I will not lay upon your blushing and delicate cheek any other colours than such as will give luster to your chitty faces. In and to that purpose, our thesis is taken out of that most plentiful but most precious book, entitled the Economical Cornucopia.

FIRST COURTESAN
The what?

LAZARILLO
The Economical Cornucopia. Thus,
"Wise is that wife who with apt wit complains
That she's kept under, yet rules all the reins."

FIRST COURTESAN
Oh, again, sweet Signior. "Complains
That she's kept under?" What follows?

LAZARILLO
"Yet rules all the reins."
"Wise is that wife who with apt wit complains
That she's kept under, yet rules all the reins."
Most pure and refined plants of nature, I will not, as this distinction enticeth, take up the parts as they lie here in order: as first, to touch your wisdom, it were folly; next, your complaining, 'tis too common; thirdly, your keeping under, 'tis above my capacity; and lastly, the reins in your own hands, that is the a-per-se of all, the very cream of all, and therefore how to skim off that only, only listen: a wife wise, no matter; apt wit, no matter; complaining, no matter; kept under, no great matter; but to rule the roast, is the matter.

THIRD COURTESAN
That ruling of the roast goes with me.

FOURTH COURTESAN
And me.

FIFTH COURTESAN
And me; I'll have a cut of that roast.

LAZARILLO
Since then a woman's only desire is to have the reins in her own white hand, your chief practice, the very same day that you are wived, must be to get hold of these reins, and being fully gotten, or wound about, "yet to complain with apt wit as tho' you had them not."

IMPERIA
How shall we know, signior, when we have them all or not?

LAZARILLO
I will furnish your capable understandings, out of my poor Spanish store, with the chief implements and their appurtenances. Observe: it shall be your first and finest praise to sing the note of every new fashion at first sight, and if you can, to stretch that note above ela.

OMNES
Good.

LAZARILLO
The more you pinch your servants' bellies for this, the smoother will the fashion sit on your back; but if your goodman like not this music, as being too full of crochets, your only way is to learn to play upon the virginals, and so nail his ears to your sweet humours. If this be out of time too, yet your labour will quit the cost, for by this means your secret friend may have free and open access to you under the colour of pricking you lessons. Now, because you may tie your husband's love in most sweet knots, you shall never give over labouring, till out of his purse you have digged a garden; and that garden must stand a pretty distance from the chitty, for by repairing thither, much good fruit may be grafted.

FIRST COURTESAN
Mark that.

LAZARILLO
Then, in the afternoon, when you address your sweet perfum'd body to walk to this garden, there to gather a nosegay, sops-in-wine, cowslips, columbines, heart's-ease, etc., the first principle to learn is that you stick black patches for the rheum on your delicate blue temples, tho' there be no room for the rheum. Black patches are comely in most women, and being well-fastened, draw men's eyes to shoot glances at you. Next, your ruff must stand in print, and for that purpose, get poking-sticks with fair and long handles, lest they scorch your lily sweating hands. Then your hat with a little brim, if you have a little face; if otherwise, otherwise. Besides, you must play the wag with your wanton fan; have your dog (call'd Pearl or Min or Why ask you, or any other pretty name) dance along by you; your embroidered muff before you on your ravishing hands, but take heed who thrusts his fingers into your fur.

SECOND COURTESAN
We'll watch for that.

LAZARILLO
Once a quarter, take state upon you and be chick; being chick, thus politicly, lie at your garden. Your lip-sworn servant may there visit you as a physician; where otherwise, if you languish at home, be sure your husband will look to your water. This chickness may be increas'd with giving out that you breed young bones, and to stick flesh upon those bones, it shall not be amiss if you long for peascods, at ten groats the cod, and for cherries at a crown the cherry.

FIRST COURTESAN
O dear tutor!

SECOND COURTESAN
Interrupt him not.

LAZARILLO
If, while this pleasing fit of chickness hold you, you be invited forth to supper, whimper and seem unwilling to go; but if your goodman, bestowing the sweet duck and kiss upon your moist lip, entreat, go. Marry, my counsel is, you eat little at table, because it may be said of you you are no cormorant; yet at your coming home you may counterfeit a qualm, and so devour a posset. Your husband need not have his nose in that posset; no, trust your chambermaid only in this, and scarcely her, for you cannot be too careful into whose hands you commit your secrets.

OMNES
That's certain.

LAZARILLO
If you have daughters capable, marry them by no means to chittizens, but choose for them some smooth-chinned, curl'd-headed gentleman, for gentlemen will lift up your daughters to their own content; and to make these curl'd-pated gallants come off the more roundly, make your husband go to the herald for arms, and let it be your daily care that he have a fair and comely crest. Yea, go all the ways yourselves you can to be made ladies, especially if, without danger to his person, or for love or money, you can procure your husband to be dubbed. The goddess of memory lock up these jewels, which I have bestowed upon you, in your sweet brains; let these be the rules to square out your life by, tho' you ne'er go level, but tread your shoes awry. If you can get these reins into your lily hand, you shall need no coaches but may drive your husband's. Put it down, and according to that wise saying of you, be saints in the church, angels in the street, devils in the kitchen, and apes in your bed. Upon which, leaving you tumbling, pardon me that thus abruptly and openly I take you all up.

FIRST COURTESAN
You have got so far into our books, signior, that you cannot 'scape without a pardon here, if you take us up never so snappishly.

IMPERIA
Music there to close our stomachs. How do you like him, madonna?

SECOND COURTESAN
O, trust me, I like him most profoundly. Why, he's able to put down twenty such as I am.

THIRD COURTESAN

Let them build upon that. Nay, more, we'll henceforth never go to a cunning woman, since men can teach us our lerry.

FOURTH COURTESAN
We are all fools to him, and our husbands, if we can hold these reins fast, shall be fools to us.

FIFTH COURTESAN
If we can keep but this bias, wenches, our goodmen may perchance once in a month get a foregame of us; but if they win a rubbers, let them throw their caps at it.

IMPERIA
No, no, no, dear features, hold their noses to the grindstone and they're gone. Thanks, worthy signior. Fie, fie, fie, you stand bare too long. Come, bright mirrors, will you withdraw into a gallery and taste a slight banquet?

FIRST COURTESAN
We shall cloy ourselves with sweets, my sweet madonna.

SECOND COURTESAN
Troth, I will not, Madonna Imperia.

IMPERIA
No, no, no, fie, fie, fie! Signior Lazarillo; either be you our foreman, or else put in these ladies at your discretion into the gallery and cut off this striving.

LAZARILLO
It shall be my office, my fees being, as they pass, to take toll of their alablaster hands.

Exeunt COURTESANS. IMPERIA, along with SIMPERINA].

Admired creature, I summon you to a parley; you remember this is the night?

IMPERIA
So, so, so, I do remember. Here is a key, that is your chamber. Lights, Simperina. About twelve a' clock you shall take my beauty prisoner. Fie, fie, fie, how I blush. At twelve a' clock.

LAZARILLO
Rich argosy of all golden pleasure!

IMPERIA
No, no, no, put up, put up your joys till anon; I will come, by my virginity. But I must tell you one thing, that all my chambers are many nights haunted, with what sprites none can see; but sometimes we hear birds singing, sometimes music playing, sometimes voices laughing. But stir not you, nor be frighted at anything.

LAZARILLO
By Hercules, if any spirits rise, I will conjure them in their own circles with toledo.

IMPERIA
So, so, so; lights for his chamber. [To SIMPERINA] Is the trapdoor ready?

SIMPERINA
'Tis set sure.

IMPERIA
So, so, so, I will be rid of this broiled red sprat that stinks so in my stomach, fih. I hate him worse than to have a tailor come a-wooing to me. [To LAZARILLO] God's me, the sweet ladies, the banquet, I forget. Fie, fie, follow, dear signior. [To SIMPERINA] The trapdoor, Simperina.

Exit.

SIMPERINA
Signior, come away.

LAZARILLO
Cupid, I kiss the nock of thy sweet bow!
A woman makes me yield; Mars could not so.

Exeunt.

ACT IV

SCENE I. A Street Before Imperia's House

Enter CURVETTO with a lantern.

CURVETTO
Just ten? 'Tis ten just: that's the fixed hour
For payment of my love's due fees; that broke,
I forfeit a huge sum of joys. Ho love!
I'll keep time just to a minute, ay;
A sweet guide's loss is a deep penalty.
A night's so rich a venture to taste wrack,
Would make a lover bankrupt, break his back.
No, if to sit up late, early to rise,
Or if this goldfinch, that with sweet notes flies
And wakes the dull eye even of a puritan,
Can work, then wenches, Curvetto is the man.
I am not young, yet have I youthful tricks,
Which peering day must not see; no, close, close,
Old courtier, perilous fellow. I can lie,
Hug in your bosom, close, yet none shall spy.
Stay, here's the door, the window; hah, this, this
Cord? Umh? Dear cord, thy blessed knot I kiss;

None peeps I hope. Night clap thy velvet hand
Upon all eyes! If now my friend thou stand,
I'll hang a jewel at thine ear, sweet night;
And here it is: "Lanthorne and Candlelight!";
A peal, a lusty peal, set, ring love's knell;
I'll sweat, but thus I'll bear away the bell.

Pulls the cord and is drenched with water.

Enter SIMPERINA above.

SIMPERINA
Signior? Who's there? Signior Curvetto?

CURVETTO
Umh! Drown'd? Noah's flood? Duck'd over head and ears?
O sconce! and O sconce! an old soaker, oh!
I sweat now till I drop. What villainies, oh!
Punks, punkateroes, nags, hags, I will ban.
I have catch'd my bane.

SIMPERINA
Who's there?

CURVETTO
A water-man.

SIMPERINA
Who rings that scolding peal?

CURVETTO
I am wringing wet,
I am wash'd; foh, here's rose-water sold by th' ounce.
This sconce shall batter down those windows. Bounce!

SIMPERINA
What do you mean? Why do you beat our doors?
What do you take us for?

CURVETTO
Y'are all damn'd whores!

SIMPERINA
Signior Curvetto?

CURVETTO
Signior coxcomb, no.

SIMPERINA
What makes you be so hot?

CURVETTO
You lie, I am cool;
I am an old courtier, but stinking fool!
Foh!

SIMPERINA
God's my life, what have you done? You are in a sweet pickle if you pull'd at this rope.

CURVETTO
Hang thyself in't, and I'll pull once again.

SIMPERINA
Merry muff, will you up and ride? Y'are mine elder. By my pure maidenhead, here's a jest. Why, this was a waterwork to drown a rat that uses to creep in at this window.

CURVETTO
Fire on your waterworks! Catch a drown'd rat?
That's me, I have it, God a' mercy head!
Rat? Me! I smell a rat, I strike it dead!

SIMPERINA
You smell a sodden sheep's-head. A rat? Ay, a rat! And you will not believe me, marry, foh! I have been believ'd of your betters; marry, snick up!

CURVETTO
Simp, nay, sweet Simp. Open again. Why, Simperina?

SIMPERINA
Go from my window, go; go from, etc., away. Go by, old Jeronimo; nay, and you shrink i' th' wetting. Walk, walk, walk.

CURVETTO
I cry thee mercy, if the bowl were set
To drown a rat. I shrink not, am not wet.

SIMPERINA
A rat by this hemp, and you could ha' smelt. Hark you, here's the bell; ting, ting, ting. Would the clapper were in my belly, if I am not mad at your foppery. I could scratch, fie, fie, fie, fie, fie, as my mistress says; but go, hie you home, shift you. Come back presently; here you shall find a ladder of cords. Climb up, I'll receive you. My mistress lies alone; she's yours. Away!

CURVETTO
O Simp!

SIMPERINA

Nay, scud, you know what you promis'd me. I shall have simple yawling for this; be gone and mum.

Clap the window shut, exit.

CURVETTO
Thanks, mum, dear girl; I am gone. 'Twas for a rat,
A rat upon my life. Thou shalt have gifts;
I love thee, tho' thou puts me to my shifts.
I knew I could be overreach'd by none.
A parlous head; lie close, lie close, I am gone.

Exit.

SCENE II. Lazarillo's Room in Imperia's House

Music suddenly plays, and birds sing.

Enter LAZARILLO bareheaded, in his shirt, a pair of pantaples on, a rapier in his hand and a tobacco pipe; he seems amazed, and walks so up and down.

LAZARILLO
Saint Jaques and the seven deadly sins—that is the Seven Wise Masters of the world—pardon me for this night! I will kill the devil.

WITHIN
Ha ha ha!

LAZARILLO
Thou prince of blackamoors, thou shalt have small cause to laugh if I run thee through. This chamber is haunted; would I had not been brought a bed in it, or else were well-delivered, for my heart tells me 'tis no good luck to have anything to do with the devil, he's a paltry merchant!

A song within.

Midnight's bell goes ting, ting, ting, ting, ting;
Then dogs do howl, and not a bird does sing
But the nightingale, and she cries twit, twit, twit, twit.
Owls then on every bough do sit,
Ravens croak on chimney tops,
The cricket in the chamber hops,
And the cats cry mew, mew, mew;
The nibbling mouse is not asleep,
But he goes peep, peep, peep, peep, peep;
And the cats cry mew, mew, mew,
And still the cats cry mew, mew, mew.

LAZARILLO
I shall be mous'd by puss-cats, but I had rather die a dog's death; they have nine lives apiece—like a woman—and they will make it up ten lives if they and I fall a-scratching. Bright Helena of this house, would thy Troy were a-fire, for I am a-cold; or else would I had the Greeks' wooden curtal to ride away! Most ambrosian-lipp'd creature, come away quickly, for this night's lodging lies cold at my heart.

The Spanish pavin.

The Spanish pavin! I thought the devil could not understand Spanish, but since thou art my countryman, O thou tawny Satan, I will dance after thy pipe.

He dances the Spanish pavin.

Ho, sweet devil, ho! Thou wilt make any man weary of thee, tho' he deal with thee in his shirt.
Sweet beauty, she'll not come. I'll fall to sleep,
And dream of her; love-dreams are ne'er too deep.

Falls down through a trapdoor.

Enter FRISCO above, laughing.

FRISCO
Ha, ha, ha!

LAZARILLO
Ho, ho, Frisco! Madonna! I am in hell, but here is not fire; hellfire is all put out. What ho? so, ho, ho? I shall be drown'd. I beseech thee, dear Frisco, raise Blurt the constable, or some scavenger, to come and make clean these kennels of hell, for they stink so, that I shall cast away my precious self.

Enter IMPERIA.

IMPERIA
Is he down, Frisco?

FRISCO
He's down; he cries out he's in hell. It's heaven to me to have him cry so.

IMPERIA
Fie, fie, fie; let him lie, and get all to bed.

Exit.

FRISCO
Not all; I have fatting knavery in hand.
He cries he's damn'd in hell; the next shall cry
He's climbing up to heaven, and here's the gin:
One woodcock's ta'en; I'll have his brother in.

Exit.

SCENE III. A Street Before Imperia's House, A Rope Ladder Hanging From the Window

Enter CURVETTO.

CURVETTO
Brisk as a cap'ring tailor! I was wash'd,
But did they shave me? No, I am too wise.
Lie close i' th' bosom of their knaveries;
I am an old hoary courtier, and strike dead.
I hit my marks; 'ware, 'ware, a perilous head.
Cast: I must find a ladder made of ropes.

Enter BLURT and watch.

Ladder and rope; what follow? Hanging. Ay,
But where? Ah ha, there does the riddle lie!
I have 'scap'd drowning, but, but, but I hope
I shall not 'scape the ladder and the rope.

WOODCOCK
Yonder's a light, master constable.

BLURT
Peace, Woodcock, the sconce approaches.

CURVETTO
Whew!

BLURT
Ay, whistling? Slubber, jog the watch and give the lanthorn a slap.

CURVETTO
Whew, Simp, Simp?

Enter FRISCO above.

FRISCO
Who's there?

CURVETTO
Who's there?

FRISCO

Signior Curvetto, here's the ladder. I watch to do you a good turn. I am Frisco. Is not Blurt abroad and his bill-men?

CURVETTO
No matter if they be; I hear none nigh.
I will snug close; out goes my candle's eye.
My sconce takes this in snuff; all's one, I care not.

FRISCO
Why, when?

CURVETTO
I come, close, close; hold, rope and spare not.

[Begins to ascend ladder.

SLUBBER
Now the candle's out.

BLURT
Peace.

CURVETTO
Frisco, light, light! My foot is slipp'd; call help!

FRISCO
Help, help, help! Thieves, thieves! Help, thieves, etc.

BLURT
Thieves? Where? Follow close: Slubber, the lanthorn! [To CURVETTO] Hold! I charge you in the duke's name, stand. Sirrah, y'are like to hang for this. Down with him.

They take him down.

FRISCO
Master Blurt, master constable, here's his ladder; he comes to rob my mistress. I have been scar'd out of my wits above seven times by him and it's forty to one if ever they come in again. I lay felony to his charge.

CURVETTO
Felony? You cony-catching slave!

FRISCO
Cony-catching will bear an action; I'll cony-catch you for this. If I can find our key, I will aid you, Master Blurt; if not, look to him as you will answer it upon your deathbed.

BLURT
What are you?

CURVETTO
A Venetian gentleman. Woodcock? How dost thou, Woodcock?

WOODCOCK
Thank your worship.

BLURT
Woodcock, you are of our side now, and therefore your acquaintance cannot serve; and you were a gentleman of velvet, I would commit you.

CURVETTO
Why, what are you, sir?

BLURT
What am I, sir? Do not you know this staff? I am, sir, the duke's own image; at this time the duke's tongue, for fault of a better, lies in my mouth. I am constable, sir.

CURVETTO
Constable, and commit me? Marry, Blurt, master constable!

BLURT
Away with him!

He strives.

OMNES
It's folly to strive.

BLURT
I say away with him! [To CURVETTO] I'll Blurt you; I'll teach you to stand cover'd to authority. Your hoary head shall be knock'd when this staff is in place.

CURVETTO
Ay, but master constable—

BLURT
No, pardon me, you abuseth the duke in me, that am his cipher. [To watch] I say away with him! Gulch, away with him; Woodcock, keep you with me. I will be known for more than Blurt.

Exeunt BLURT and the watch with CURVETTO.

Enter LAZARILLO.

LAZARILLO
Thou honest fellow, the man in the moon, I beseech thee set fire on thy bush of thorns to light and warm me, for I am dung-wet. I fell like Lucifer, I think, into hell, and am crawl'd out, but in worse pickle than my lean Pilcher. Hereabout is the hothouse of my love. Ho, ho; why, ho there!

FRISCO
Who's that? What devil stands ho-ing at my door so late?

LAZARILLO
I beseech thee, Frisco, take in Lazarillo's ghost.

FRISCO
Lazarillo's ghost? Haunt me not, I charge thee. I know thee not. I am in a dream of a dry summer, therefore appear not to me.

LAZARILLO
Is not this the mansion of the cherry-lipp'd Madonna Imperia?

FRISCO
Yes; how then? You fly-blown rascal, what art thou?

LAZARILLO
Lazarillo de Tormes. Sweet blood, I have a poor Spanish suit depending in your house. Let me enter, most precious Frisco; the mistress of this mansion is my beautiful hostess.

FRISCO
How? You turpentine pill, my wife your hostess? Away, you Spanish vermin!

LAZARILLO
I beseech thee, most pitiful Frisco, allow my lamentation.

FRISCO
And you lament here, I'll stone you with brickbats; I am asleep.

LAZARILLO
My slop and mandillion lie at thy mercy, fine Frisco. I beseech thee, let not my case be thine; I must and will lament.

FRISCO
Must you? I'll wash off your tears! Away, you hog's-face!

[Drenches him with urine, then exit.

LAZARILLO
Thou hast soused my poor hog's-face. O Frisco, thou art a scurvy doctor to cast my water no better; it is a most rammish urine. Mars shall not save thee; I will make a brown toast of thy heart, and drink it in a pot of thy strong blood!

Enter BLURT and all his watch.

BLURT
Such fellows must be taken down. Stand; what white thing is yonder?

SLUBBER
Who goes there? Come before the constable.

LAZARILLO
My dear host Blurt.

BLURT
You have blurted fair; I am by my office to examine you. Where have you spent these two nights?

LAZARILLO
Most big Blurt, I answer thy great authority that I have been in hell, and am scratch'd to death with puss-cats.

BLURT
Do you run a' th' score at an officer's house, and then run above twelve score off?

LAZARILLO
I did not run, my sweet-fac'd Blurt: the Spanish fleet is bringing gold enough to discharge all, from the Indies. Lodge me, most pitiful bill-man!

BLURT
Marry, and will. I am in the duke's name to charge you with despicions of felony; and burglary is committed this night, and we are to reprehend any that we think to be faulty. Were not you at Madonna Freckleface's house?

LAZARILLO
Signior, sí.

BLURT
Away with him, clap him up.

LAZARILLO
Most thund'ring Blurt, do not clap me; most thund'ring Blurt, do not clap me!

BLURT
Master Lazarus, I know you are a sore fellow where you take, and therefore I charge you in the duke's name to go without wrastling, though you be in your shirt.

LAZARILLO
Commendable Blurt!

BLURT
The end of my commendations is to commit you.

LAZARILLO
I am kin to Don Dego, the Spanish adolantado.

BLURT
If you be kin to Don Dego that was smelt out in Paul's, you pack; your lantedoes nor your lanteeroes cannot serve your turn. I charge you, let me commit you to the tuition—

LAZARILLO
Worshipful Blurt, do not commit me into the hands of dogs.

OMNES
Dogs?

BLURT
Master Lazarus, there's not a dog shall bite you; these are true bill-men that fight under the commonwealth's flag.

LAZARILLO
Blurt—

BLURT
Blurt me no Blurts; I'll teach all Spaniards how to meddle with whores.

LAZARILLO
Most cunning constable, all Spaniards know that already; I have meddled with none.

BLURT
Your being in your shirt bewrays you.

LAZARILLO
I beseech thee, most honest Blurt, let not my shirt bewray me.

BLURT
I say, away with him!

[Music within.]

Music? That's in the courtesan's. They are about some ungodly act, but I'll play a part in't ere morning. Away with Lazarus.

OMNES
Come, Spaniard.

LAZARILLO
Thy kites and thee, for this shall watch in dirt to feed on carrion.

BLURT
Hence, ptrooh!

LAZARILLO
O base Blurt! O base Blurt! O base Blurt!

Exeunt.

ACT V

SCENE I. A Room in Camillo's House

Enter CAMILLO, HIPOLITO, VIRGILIO, ASORINO, BAPTISTA, BENTIVOLIO, DOYT and DANDIPRAT, all weapon'd, their rapiers' sheathes in their hands.

CAMILLO
Gentlemen and noble Italians, whom I love best, who know best what wrongs I have stood under, being laid on by him who is to thank me for his life. I did bestow him, as the prize of mine honour, upon my love, the most fair Violetta; my love's merit was basely sold to him by the most false Violetta. Not content with this felony, he hath dar'd to add the sweet theft of ignoble marriage. She's now none's but his, and he, treacherous villain, anyone's but her's; he dotes, my honour'd friends, on a painted courtesan, and in scorn of our Italian laws, our family, our revenge, loathes Violetta's bed, for a harlot's bosom. I conjure you therefore, by all the bonds of gentility, that as you have solemnly sworn most sharp, so let your revenge be a most sudden.

VIRGILIO
Be not yourself a bar to that suddenness by this protraction.

OMNES
Away, gentlemen, away then.

HIPOLITO
As for that light hobbyhorse, my sister, whose foul name I will rase out with my poniard, by the honour of my family, which her lust hath profaned, I swear—and gentlemen, be in this my sworn brothers—I swear that as all Venice does admire her beauty, so all the world shall be amazed at her punishment. Follow, therefore.

VIRGILIO
Stay, let our resolutions keep together; whither go we first?

CAMILLO
To the strumpet Imperia's.

OMNES
Agreed; what then?

CAMILLO
There to find Fontinell; found, to kill him.

VIRGILIO
And kill'd, to hang out his reeking body at his harlot's window.

CAMILLO
And by his body, the strumpet's.

HIPOLITO
And between both, my sister's.

VIRGILIO
The tragedy is just. On then; begin.

CAMILLO
As you go, every hand pull in a friend to strengthen us against all opposites; he that has any drop of true Italian blood in him, thus vow this morning to shed others', or let out his own. If you consent to this, follow me.

OMNES
Via, away! The treacherous Frenchman dies!

HIPOLITO
Catso, Saint Mark, my pistol; thus death flies.

Exeunt.

SCENE II. A Room in Imperia's House

Enter FONTINELL and IMPERIA arm in arm.

IMPERIA
Ah, you little effeminate sweet chevalier, why does thou not get a loose periwig of hair on thy chin to set thy French face off? By the panting pulse of Venus, thou art welcome a thousand degrees beyond the reach of arithmetic. Good, good, good, your lip is moist and moving; it hath the truest French close, even like, "Mapew, la, la, la, etc."

FONTINELL
Dear lady, O life of love, what sweetness dwells
In love's variety! The soul that plods
In one harsh book of beauty but repeats
The stale and tedious learning that hath oft
Faded the senses, when in reading more
We glide in new sweets, and are starv'd with store.
Now, by the heart of love, my Violet
Is a foul weed, O pure Italian flower!
She a black negro to the white compare
Of this unequal'd beauty? O most accurst,
That I have given her leave to challenge me!
But, lady, poison speaks Italian well,

And in a loathed kiss I'll include her hell.

IMPERIA
So, so, so; do, do, do. Come, come, come, will you condemn the mute rushes to be press'd to death by your sweet body? Down, down, down, here, here, here; lean your head upon the lap of my gown. Good, good, good. O Saint Mark, here is a love-mark able to wear more ladies' eyes for Jewels than— Oh! Lie still, lie still; I will level a true Venetian kiss over your right shoulder.

FONTINELL
Shoot home, fair mistress, and as that kiss flies
From lip to lip, wound me with your sharp eyes.

IMPERIA
No, no, no, I'll beat this cherry tree thus, and thus, and thus, and you name wound.

Kiss him.

FONTINELL
I will offend so, to be beaten still.

IMPERIA
Do, do, do, and if you make any more such lips when I beat you, by my virginity, you shall buss this rod. Music, I pray thee be not a puritan. Sister to the rest of the sciences, I knew the time when thou couldst abide handling.

Loud music.

Oh fie, fie, fie, forbear! Thou art like a puny barber, new come to the trade: thou pick'st our ears too deep. So, so, so; will my sweet prisoner entertain a poor Italian song?

FONTINELL
O, most willingly, my dear madonna.

IMPERIA
I care not if I persuade my bad voice to wrastle with this music and catch a strain; so, so, so, keep time, keep time, keep time.

Song.

Love for such a cherry lip
Would be glad to pawn his arrows;
Venus here to take a sip
Would sell her doves and team of sparrows.
But they shall not so,
Hey nonny nonny no:
None but I this lip must owe,
Hey nonny nonny no.

FONTINELL
Your voice does teach the music.

IMPERIA
No, no, no.

FONTINELL
Again, dear love.

IMPERIA: Hey nonny nonny no.
Did Jove see this wanton eye,
Ganymede must wait no longer;
Phoebe here one night did lie,
Would change her face and look much younger.
But they shall not so,
Hey nonny nonny no;
None but I this lip must owe,
Hey nonny nonny no—

Enter FRISCO, TRIVIA, and SIMPERINA running.

OMNES
O Madonna! Mistress! Madonna!

FRISCO
Case up this gentleman; there's rapping at door, and one in a small voice says there's Camillo and Hipolito.

SIMPERINA
And they will come in.

FONTINELL
Upon their deaths they shall, for they seek mine.

IMPERIA
No, no, no; lock the doors fast! Trivia, Simperina, stir!

BOTH
Alas!

FONTINELL
Come they in shape of devils this angel by,
I am arm'd; let them come in. 'Uds foot, they die!

IMPERIA
Fie, fie, fie, I will not have thy white body—

Knock.

VIOLETTA
[Within] What ho, madonna?

IMPERIA
O hark! Not hurt, for the Rialto! Go, go, go, put up; by my virginity, put up!

VIOLETTA
[Within] Here are Camillo and Hipolito.

IMPERIA
Into that little room; you are there as safe as in France or the Low Countries.

FONTINELL
Oh God!

Exit.

IMPERIA
So, so, so, let them enter.

Exit FRISCO.

Trivia, Simperina, smooth my gown, tread down the rushes. Let them enter, do, do, do; no words, pretty darling. [Singing] La, la, la, hey nonny nonny no!

Enter FRISCO and VIOLETTA.

FRISCO
Are two men transformed into one woman?

IMPERIA
How now? What motion's this?

VIOLETTA
By your leave, sweet beauty, pardon my excuse which under the mask of Camillo's and my brother's names sought entrance into this house. Good sweetness, have you not a property here, improper to your house: my husband?

IMPERIA
Hah, your husband here?

VIOLETTA
Nay, be as you seem to be, white dove, without gall.

IMPERIA
Gall? Your husband? Ha ha ha! By my ventoy, yellow lady, you take your mark improper. No, no, no, my sugar-candy mistress, your goodman is not here, I assure you. Here? Ha ha!

TRIVIA and SIMPERINA
Here?

FRISCO
Much husbands here!

VIOLETTA
Do not mock me, fairest Venetian. Come, I know he's here. Good faith, I do not blame him, for your beauty glides over his error. Troth, I am right glad that you, my countrywoman, have received the pawn of my affections; you cannot be hard-hearted loving him, nor hate me, for I love him too. Since we both love him, let us not leave him till we have call'd home the ill husbandry of a sweet straggler. Prithee, good wench, use him well.

IMPERIA
So, so, so.

VIOLETTA
If he deserve not to be used well (as I'd be loath he should deserve it), I'll engage myself, dear beauty, to thine honest heart. Give me leave to love him and I'll give him a kind of leave to love thee. I know he hears me; I prithee, try mine eyes if they know him, that have almost drown'd themselves in their own salt water because they cannot see him. In troth, I'll not chide him; if I speak words rougher than soft kisses, my penance shall be to see him kiss thee, yet to hold my peace.

FRISCO
And that's torment enough; alas, poor wench.

SIMPERINA
She's an ass, by the crown of my maidenhead; I'd scratch her eyes out if my man stood in her tables.

VIOLETTA
Good partner, lodge me in thy private bed,
Where in supposed folly he may end
Determin'd sin. Thou smil'st; I know thou wilt.
What looseness may term dotage, truly read,
Is love ripe-gather'd, not soon withered.

IMPERIA
Good troth, pretty wedlock, thou mak'st my little eyes smart with washing themselves in brine. I keep your cock from his own roost? and mar such a sweet face? and wipe off that dainty red? and make Cupid toll the bell for your love-sick heart? No, no, no, if he were Jove's own ingle, Ganymede; fie, fie, fie, I'll none. Your chamber-fellow is within; thou shalt enjoy my bed, and thine own pleasure this night. Simperina, conduct in this lady. [Aside, to Frisco] Frisco, silence. Ha ha ha! I am sorry to see a woman so tame a fool. Come, come, come.

VIOLETTA
Star of Venetian beauty, thanks; O, who
Can bear this wrong, and be a woman too?

Exeunt.

SCENE III. A Street Before Imperia's House

Enter CAMILLO, HIPOLITO, VIRGILIO and others, the DUKE and GENTLEMEN with him, BLURT and his watch on his side, with torches.

OMNES
We are dishonour'd! Give us way! He dies, he dies!

DUKE
I charge you, by your duties to the state,
And love to gentry, sheathe your weapons.

BLURT
Stand! I charge you put up your naked weapons, and we'll put up our rusty bills.

CAMILLO
Up to the hilts we will in his French body.
My lord, we charge you by the ravish'd honour
Of an Italian lady, by our wrongs,
By that eternal blot, which, if this slave
Pass free without revenge, like leprosy
Will run over all the body of our fames,
Give open way to our just wrath, lest barr'd—

DUKE
Gentlemen—

CAMILLO
Breaking the bonds of honour and of duty,
We cut a passage through you with our swords.

OMNES
He that withstands us, run him through!

BLURT
I charge you, i' th' duke's name, before his own face, to keep the peace.

CAMILLO
Keep thou the peace, that hast a peasant's heart.

WATCH
Peasant?

CAMILLO
Our peace must have her cheeks painted with blood.

OMNES
Away, through—

BLURT
Sweet gentlemen, though you have called the duke's own ghost peasant, for I walk for him i' th' night—Kilderkin and Pissbreech, hold out—yet hear me, dear bloods: the duke here for fault of a better and myself—Cuckoo, fly not hence—for fault of a better, are to lay you by the heels if you go thus with fire and sword, for the duke is the head, and I, Blurt, am the purtenance. Woodcock, keep by my side. Now sir—

OMNES
A plague upon this Woodcock; kill the watch!

DUKE
Now, in the name of manhood, I conjure ye,
Appear in your true shapes; Italians,
You kill your honours more in this revenge
Than in his murder. Stay, stand; here's the house.

BLURT
Right, sir, this is the whorehouse; here he calls and sets in his staff.

DUKE
Sheathe all your weapons, worthy gentlemen,
And by my life I swear, if Fontinell
Have stain'd the honour of your sister's bed,
The fact being death, I'll pay you his proud head.

CAMILLO
Arrest him then before our eyes, and see,
Our fury sleeps.

DUKE
This honest officer—

BLURT
Blurt, sir.

DUKE
Shall fetch him forth. [To BLURT] Go, sirrah, in our name;
Attach the French lord.

BLURT
Garlic and the rest, follow strongly.

Exeunt BLURT and the watch.

DUKE
O, what a scandal were it to a state,
To have a stranger, and a prisoner,
Murdered by such a troop. Besides, through Venice
Are numbers of his countrymen dispers'd,
Whose rage, meeting with yours, none can prevent
The mischief of a bloody consequent.

Enter BLURT and watch, holding FONTINELL and his weapons.

BLURT
The duke is within an inch of your nose and therefore I dare play with it, if you put not up; deliver, I advise you.

FONTINELL
Yield up my weapons, and my foe so nigh?
Myself and weapons shall together yield;
Come anyone, come all.

OMNES
Kill, kill the Frenchman! Kill him!

DUKE
Be satisfy'd, my noble countrymen.
I'll trust you with his life, so you will pawn
The faiths of gentlemen, no desperate hand
Shall rob him of it; otherwise, he runs
Upon this dangerous point, that dares appose
His rage 'gainst our authority. [To FONTINELL] French lord,
Yield up this strength; our word shall be your guard.

FONTINELL
Who defies death needs none; he's well prepared.

DUKE
My honest fellow, with good defence
Enter again; fetch out the courtesan
And all that are within.

BLURT
I'll tickle her; it shall ne'er be said that a brown bill look'd pale.

Exeunt BLURT and watch.

CAMILLO
Frenchman, thou art indebted to our duke.

FONTINELL
For what?

CAMILLO
Thy life, for but for him, thy soul
Had long ere this hung trembling in the air,
Being frighted from thy bosom with our swords.

FONTINELL
I do not thank your duke. Yet if you will,
Turn bloody executioners; who dies
For so bright beauty is a bright sacrifice.

DUKE
The beauty you adore so is profane;
The breach of wedlock by our law is death.

FONTINELL
Law! Give me law!

DUKE
With all severity.

FONTINELL
In my love's eyes immortal joys do dwell.
She is my heaven; she from me, I am in hell.
Therefore, your law, your law!

DUKE
Make way, she comes.

Enter BLURT leading IMPERIA, watch with VIOLETTA mask'd.

IMPERIA
Fie, fie, fie.

BLURT
Your fie, fie, fie, nor your foh, foh, foh, cannot serve your turn. Your must now bear it off with head and shoulders.

DUKE
Now fetch Curvetto and the Spaniard hither;
Their punishments shall lie under one doom.
What is she mask'd?

BLURT
A punk, too. [To watch] Follow, fellows; Slubber, afore.

Exeunt BLURT with the watch.

VIOLETTA
She that is mask'd is leader of this masque.
What's here? Bows, bills and guns? Unmasks Noble Camillo,
I am sure you are lord of all this misrule; I pray
For who's sake do you make this swaggering fray?

CAMILLO
For yours, and for our own, we come resolv'd
To murther him that poisons your chaste bed,
To take revenge on you for your false heart.
And, wanton dame, our wrath here must not sleep;
Your sin being deep'st, your share shall be most deep.

VIOLETTA
With pardon of your grace, myself to you all,
At your own weapons, thus do answer all.
For paying away my heart, that was my own;
Fight not to win that, in good troth, 'tis gone.
For my dear love's abusing my chaste bed
And her sweet theft, alack, you are misled;
This was a plot of mine, only to try
Your love's strange temper. Sooth, I do not lie.
My Fontinell ne'er dally'd in her arms;
She never bound his heart with amorous charms.
My Fontinell ne'er loath'd my sweet embrace;
She never drew love's picture by his face.
When he from her white hand would strive to go,
She never cry'd fie, fie, nor no, no, no.
With prayers and bribes we hired her, both to lie
Under that roof: for this must my love die?
Who dare be so hard-hearted? Look you, we kiss,
And if he loathe his Violetta, judge by this.

Kiss.

FONTINELL
O sweetest Violet, I blush.

VIOLETTA
Good sign,
Wear still that maiden blush, but still be mine.

FONTINELL
I seal myself thine own, with both my hands,
In this true deed of gift. Gallants, here stands

This lady's champion; at his foot I'll lie
That dares touch her. Who taints my constancy,
I am no man for him; fight he with her
And yield, for she's a noble conqueror.

DUKE
This combat shall not need, for see, asham'd
Of their rash vows these gentlemen here break
This storm, and do with hands what tongues should speak.

OMNES
All friends? All friends.

HIPOLITO
[To IMPERIA] Punk, you may laugh at this.
Here's tricks, but, mouth, I'll stop you with a kiss.

Enter CURVETTO and LAZARILLO, led by BLURT and the watch.

BLURT
Room; keep all the scabs back, for here comes Lazarus.

DUKE
Oh, here's our other spirits that walk i' th' night.
Signior Curvetto, by complaint from her
And by your writing here, I reach the depth
Of your offense. They charge your climbing up
To be to rob her; if so, then by law
You are to die unless she marry you.

IMPERIA
I? Fie, fie, fie, I will be burnt to ashes first.

CURVETTO
How? Die or marry her? Then call me daw.
Marry her—she's more common than the law—
For boys to call me ox? No, I am not drunk.
I'll play with her but, hang her, wed no punk.
I shall be a hoary courtier then, indeed,
And have a perilous head; then I were best
Lie close, lie close to hid my forked crest.
No; fie, fie, fie, hang me before the door
Where I was drown'd ere I marry with a whore.

DUKE
Well, signior, for we rightly understand
From your accusers how you stood her guest,
We pardon you and pass it as a jest.

And for the Spaniard sped so hardly too,
Discharge him, Blurt; signior, we pardon you.

BLURT
Sir, he's not to be dischar'd, nor so to be shot off; I have put him into a new suit and have enter'd into him with an action. He owes me two and thirty shillings.

LAZARILLO
It is thy honour to have me die in thy debt.

BLURT
It would be more honor to thee to pay me before thou diest; twenty shillings of this debt came out of his nose.

LAZARILLO
Bear witness, great duke, he's paid twenty shillings.

BLURT
Signior No, you cannot smoke me so. He took twenty shillings of it in a fume, and the rest I charge him with for his lying.

LAZARILLO
My lying, most pitiful prince, was abominable.

BLURT
He did lie, for the time, as well as any knight of the post did ever lie.

LAZARILLO
I do here put off thy suit, and appeal. I warn thee to the court of conscience, and will pay thee by two-pence a week, which I will rake out of the hot embers of tobacco ashes, and then travel on foot to the Indies for more gold, whose red cheeks I will kiss, and beat thee, Blurt, if thou watch for me.

HIPOLITO
There be many of your countrymen in Ireland, signior; travel to them.

LAZARILLO
No, I will fall no more into bogs.

DUKE
Sirrah, his debt ourself will satisfy.

BLURT
Blurt, my lord, dare take your word for as much more.

DUKE
And since this heat of fury is all spent,
And tragic shapes meet comical event,
Let this bright morning merrily be crown'd

With dances, banquets, and choice music's sound.

Exeunt.

Thomas Dekker – A Short Biography

Thomas Dekker was born around 1572, there is no certainty as to date and it is only probable that he was born in London. Little is known of his early years. From such an unknown start he was however to make quite a name for himself.

By the mid 1590s Dekker had set forth on a career as a playwright. Samples of his work (though not the actual date) can be found in the manuscript of Sir Thomas More. Of more certainty is work as a playwright for the Admiral's Men of Philip Henslowe, in whose records of account he is first mentioned in early 1598.

While there are plays connected with his name performed as early as 1594, it is not clear that he was the original author or part of a team involved in revising and updating. Much of his work has been lost and whilst his prolific output argues against any uniform quality there are undoubted gems both as a solo writer and as part of various collaborations. Indeed between 1598 and 1602, about forty plays for Henslowe, usually in collaboration, can be attributed to him.

Dekker's name first appears in Henslowe's diary* in connection with "fayeton" (presumably, Phaeton) in 1598. There follow, before 1599, payments for work on The Triplicity of Cuckolds, The Mad Man's Morris, and Hannibal and Hermes. He worked on these plays with Robert Wilson, Henry Chettle, and Michael Drayton. With Drayton, he also worked on history plays on the French civil wars, Earl Godwin, and others.

It is also recorded at this time that Dekker's long association with financial mishaps was going to be a life-long concern. He was imprisoned for a short time for debt in Poultry Compter, a small prison run by the Sherriff of London. It was used to house prisoners such as vagrants, debtors and religious dissenters, as well as criminals convicted of misdemeanours including homosexuality, prostitution and drunkenness.

In 1599, he wrote plays on Troilus and Cressida, Agamemnon (with Chettle), and Page of Plymouth. In that year, also, he collaborated with Chettle, Jonson, and Marston on a play about Robert II.

1599 also saw the production of three plays that have survived including his most famous work, The Shoemaker's Holiday, or the Gentle Craft. This play reflects the daily lives of ordinary Londoners, and contains the poem The Merry Month of May. The play reflects the trend for the intermingling of everyday subjects with the fantastical, embodied here by the rise of a craftsman to Mayor and the involvement of an unnamed but idealised king in the concluding banquet. Old Fortunatus and Patient Grissel are the two other surviving plays.

In 1600, he worked on The Seven Wise Masters, Fortune's Tennis, Cupid and Psyche, and Fair Constance of Rome. The next year, in addition to the classic Satiromastix, he worked on a play possibly about Sebastian of Portugal and Blurt, Master Constable, on which he may have collaborated with Thomas Middleton.

To these years also belong the collaborations with Ben Jonson and John Marston, which presumably contributed to the War of the Theatres in 1600 and 1601. To Jonson, Dekker was a hack, a "dresser of plays about town"; Jonson made fun of Dekker as Demetrius Fannius in Poetaster and as Anaides in Cynthia's Revels.

Dekker's riposte, Satiromastix, performed both by the Lord Chamberlain's Men and the child actors of Paul's, casts Jonson as an affected, hypocritical Horace and marks the end of the "poetomachia".

In 1602 he revised two older plays, Pontius Pilate (1597) and the second part of Sir John Oldcastle. He also collaborated on Caesar's Fall, Jephthah, A Medicine for a Curst Wife, Sir Thomas Wyatt (on Wyatt's rebellion), and Christmas Comes But Once a Year.

By 1603, Jonson and Dekker collaborated again, on a pageant for the Royal Entry, delayed from the coronation of James I, for which Dekker also wrote the festival book The Magnificent Entertainment.

At this point Dekker becomes more interested in writing pamphlets; he had done so from the start of his career but now increases his work flow and his playwriting output noticeably declines. It appears also that his association with Henslowe also breaks at this point.

In Dekker's first rush of pamphleteering, in 1603, was The Wonderful Year, a journalistic account of the death of Elizabeth, accession of James I, and the 1603 plague, that combined a wide variety of literary styles to convey the extraordinary events of that year ('wonderful' here meaning astonishing). Its reception prompted two more plague pamphlets, News From Gravesend and The Meeting of Gallants at an Ordinary. The Double PP (1606) is an anti-Catholic tract written in response to the Gunpowder Plot. News From Hell (1606) is an homage to and continuation of Nash's Pierce Penniless. The Seven Deadly Sins of London (1606) continues the plague pamphlet series.

In 1604, he and Middleton wrote The Honest Whore for the Fortune, and Dekker contributed a sequel himself the following year. The Middleton/Dekker collaboration The Family of Love also dates from this time. Dekker and Webster also wrote Westward Ho and Northward Ho for Paul's Boys.

The failures of The Whore of Babylon (1607) and If This Be Not a Good Play, the Devil is in It (1611) left him crestfallen; the latter play was rejected by Prince Henry's Men before failing for Queen Anne's Men at the Red Bull Theatre.

After 1608, Dekker produced his most popular pamphlets: a series of "cony-catching" pamphlets that described the various tricks and deceits of confidence-men and thieves, including Thieves' Cant. These pamphlets, which Dekker often updated and reissued, include The Belman of London (1608, now The Bellman of London), Lanthorne and Candle-light, Villainies Discovered by Candlelight, and English Villainies. They owe their form and many of their incidents to similar pamphlets by Robert Greene.

Other pamphlets are journalistic in form and offer vivid pictures of Jacobean London. The Dead Term (1608) describes Westminster during summer vacation. The Guls Horne-Booke (1609, now The Gull's Hornbook) describes the life of city gallants, with a valuable account of behaviour in the London theatres. Work for Armourers (1609) and The Artillery Garden (1616) (the latter in verse) describe aspects of England's military industries. London Look Back (1630) treats 1625, the year of James's death, while Wars, Wars, Wars (1628) describes European turmoil.

The Roaring Girl, a city comedy that using the real-life figure 'Moll Cutpurse', aka Mary Frith, was another collaboration with Middleton in 1611. The same year, he wrote another tragicomedy; Match Me in London.

In 1612, Dekker's lifelong problem with debt reached a crisis point when he was imprisoned in the King's Bench Prison on a debt of forty pounds to the father of John Webster. He remained there for seven years and continued writing pamphlets during these years but wrote no plays. He did however contribute six prison-based sketches to the sixth edition (1616) of Sir Thomas Overbury's Characters; and he revised Lanthorne and Candlelight to reflect what he had learned in prison.

Dekker also wrote a long poem Dekker His Dreame (1620) cataloguing his despairing confinement;

After his release, he collaborated with Day on Guy of Warwick (1620), The Wonder of a Kingdom (1623), and The Bellman of Paris (1623). He also wrote the tragicomedy The Noble Spanish Soldier (1622) and later reworked material from this play into a comedic form to produce The Welsh Ambassador (1623).

With John Ford, he wrote The Sun's Darling (1624), The Fairy Knight (1624), and The Bristow Merchant (1624).

Another play, The Late Murder of the Son upon the Mother, or Keep the Widow Waking (with Ford, Webster, and William Rowley) dramatized two recent murders in Whitechapel, and resulted in a suit for slander heard in the Star Chamber.

Dekker turned once more to pamphlet-writing, revamping old work and writing a new preface to his most popular tract, The Bellman of London.

Dekker's plays of the 1620s were staged at the large amphitheaters on the north side of London, most commonly at the Red Bull; only two of his later plays were seen at the more exclusive, indoor Cockpit Theatre. The Shoreditch amphitheaters had become identified with the louder, less reputable play-goers, such as apprentices. Dekker's type of play seems to have suited them perfectly. Full of bold action and complementary to the values and beliefs of such audiences, his drama carried much of the thrusting optimism of Elizabethan drama into the Caroline era.

Dekker published no more work after 1632, and he it is thought he died on August 25th, 1632, recorded as "Thomas Dekker, householder". He is buried at St. James's in Clerkenwell.

Most of Dekker's work is lost. His disordered life, and his lack of a firm connection (such as Shakespeare had) with a single company, may have hindered the preservation or publication of manuscripts although perhaps twenty of his plays were published during his lifetime.

*Henslowe's diary
Philip Henslowe was an Elizabethan theatrical entrepreneur and impresario although he had a wide range of other business interests. Henslowe's reputation rests on the survival of his diary, a primary source for information about the theatrical world of Renaissance London.

Henslowe's "diary" is a valuable source on the theatrical history of the period. It is a collection of memoranda and notes that record payments to writers, box office takings, and lists of money lent. Also of interest are records of the purchase of expensive costumes and of stage properties, such as the dragon in Christopher Marlowe's Doctor Faustus, providing an insight into the staging of plays in the Elizabethan theatre.

The diary is written on the reverse of pages of a book of accounts of his brother-in-law Ralf Hogge's ironworks, kept by his brother John Henslowe for the period 1576–1581. Hogge was the Queen's Gunstone maker, and produced both iron cannon and shot for the Royal Armouries at the Tower of London. John Henslowe seems to have acted as his agent, and Philip to have prudently reused his old account book. Hence these entries are also a valuable source for the early iron-making industry.

The diary begins with Henslowe's theatrical activities for 1592. Entries, with varying degrees of detail (authors' names were not included before 1597), until 1609. In the years before his death, Henslowe appears to have run his theatrical interests from a greater distance.

The diary records payments to twenty-seven Elizabethan playwrights. He variously commissioned, bought and produced plays by, or made loans to Ben Jonson, Christopher Marlowe, Thomas Middleton, Robert Greene, Henry Chettle, George Chapman, Thomas Dekker, John Webster, Anthony Munday, Henry Porter, John Day, John Marston and Michael Drayton. The diary reveals the varying partnerships between writers, in an age when many plays were collaborations. It also shows Henslowe to have been a careful man of business, obtaining security in the form of rights to his authors' works, and holding their manuscripts, while tying them to him with loans and advances. If a play was successful, Henslowe would commission a sequel.

Performances of works with titles similar to Shakespearean plays, such as a Hamlet, a Henry VI, Part 1, a Henry V, a The Taming of the Shrew and a Titus Andronicus are mentioned in the diary with no author listed. Most of these plays were recorded when the Admiral's Men and the Lord Chamberlain's Men briefly joined forces when the playhouses were closed owing to the plague (June 1594).

In 1599, Henslowe paid Dekker and Henry Chettle for a play called Troilus and Cressida, which is probably the play currently known as British Museum MS. Add 10449 (the actors' names that appear in the plot connect it to the Admiral's Men and date it between March 1598 and July 1600). There is no mention of William Shakespeare (or for that matter Richard Burbage) in Henslowe's diary (despite the forgeries of John Payne Collier), this is due to the fact that Shakespeare and Burbage were during most of their career not connected to Henslowe's theatre, Shakespeare's company, the Lord Chamberlain's Men, performed at The Theatre (starting in 1594) and later The Globe Theatre (starting in 1599).

Thomas Dekker – A Concise Bibliography

Plays – Sole Authorship
The Shoemaker's Holiday (1599)
Old Fortunatus (1600)
The Noble Spanish Soldier (1602)
Troja-Nova Triumphans, or London Triumphing (1612)
London's Tempe; or, The Feild of Happines (1629)

The Honest Whore, Part II (1630)
Match Me in London (1631)
The Wonder of a Kingdom (1634)

Plays – Co-Written
Satiro-Mastix (1601) with Marston
Blurt, Master Constable (1602) with Middleton
Patient Grissill (1603) with Chettle and Haughton
The Honest Whore, Part I (1604) with Middleton
The Magnificent Entertainment (1604) with Jonson et al.
The Family of Love (1603-1607) with Middleton
Northward Ho (1607) with Webster
Westward Ho (1607) with Webster
The Famous History of Sir Thomas Wyatt (1607) with Webster
The Roaring Girl (1610) with Middleton
The Witch of Edmonton (1621) with Ford, Rowley, &c.
The Virgin-Martyr (1622) with Massinger
The Sun's Darling (1623-4) with Ford
The Bloody Banquet (1639) with Middleton

Non-Dramatic Works
The Wonderful Year (1603)
News from Hell (1606)
The Double PP (1606)
The Seven Deadly Sins of London (1606)
Jests to Make You Merry (1607)
The Bellman of London (1608)
Lanthorne and Candle-light (1608)
The Dead Term (1608)
The Gull's Hornbook (1609)
The Four Birds of Noah's Ark (1609)
The Raven's Almanack (1609)
Work for Armourers (1609)
O Per Se O (1612)
A Strange Horse-Race (1613)
Dekker, His Dreame (1620)
A Rod for Runaways (1625)

Poems
Golden Slumbers Kiss Your Eyes
Beauty Arise
Cast Away Care
The Invitation
Fancies Are But Streams
Here Lies The Blithe Spring

www.ingramcontent.com/pod-product-compliance
Lightning Source LLC
Chambersburg PA
CBHW071412040426
42444CB00009B/2211